COGAT® TEST PREP

Level 11

Gateway Gifted Resources™

www.GatewayGifted.com

PLEASE LEAVE US
A REVIEW!

Thank you for selecting this book. We are a family-owned publishing company - a consortium of educators, test designers, book designers, parents, and kid-testers.

We would be thrilled if you left us a quick review on the website where you purchased this book!

The Gateway Gifted Resources™ Team
www.GatewayGifted.com

TABLE OF CONTENTS

ABOUT THIS BOOK: This book helps prepare children for the COGAT® Level 11, a test given to fifth graders. Not only will this publication help prepare children for the COGAT®, these logic-based exercises may also be used for other gifted test preparation and as critical thinking exercises. This book has five parts.

1. **Introduction (p.4-9):** About this book & the COGAT®, Test Taking Tips, and Question Examples

2. **Practice Test 1 (Workbook Format):** These pages are designed similarly to content tested in the COGAT®'s nine test question types. Unless your child already has experience with COGAT® prep materials, you should complete Practice Test 1 (Workbook Format) together with no time limit. **Before doing this section with your child, read the Question Examples & Explanations (p.5).**

3. **Practice Test 2:** Practice Test 2 helps children develop critical thinking and test-taking skills. It provides an introduction to standardized testing in a relaxed manner (parents provide guidance if needed) and an opportunity for children to focus on a group of questions for a longer time period (something to which some children are not accustomed). This part is also a way for parents to identify points of strength/ weakness in COGAT® question types. Practice Test 2 is divided into three sections to mirror the three COGAT® batteries: Verbal, Quantitative, and Non-Verbal.

4. **Answer Keys:** These pages contain the Practice Test answers as well as brief answer explanations.

5. Bubble Sheet for Practice Test 2

ABOUT THE COGAT® LEVEL 11: The COGAT® (Cognitive Abilities Test®) test is divided into 3 "batteries."

- *Verbal Battery; total time: around 45 minutes*

Question Types (15 minutes each, approximately): Verbal Analogies, Verbal Classification, Sentence Completion

- *Non-Verbal Battery; total time: around 45 minutes*

Question Types (15 minutes each, approximately): Figure Analogies, Figure Classification, Paper Folding

- *Quantitative Battery; total time: around 45 minutes*

Question Types (15 minutes each, approximately): Number Series, Number Puzzles, Number Analogies

The test has 176 questions total. The test is administered in different testing sessions. Children are not expected to finish 176 questions in one session.

ABOUT COGAT® TESTING PROCEDURES: These vary by school. Tests may be given individually or in a group. These tests may be used as the single factor for admission to gifted programs, or they may be used in combination with IQ tests or as part of a student "portfolio." They are used by some schools together with tests like Iowa Assessments™. Check with your testing site to determine its specific testing procedures.

QUESTION NOTE: Because each child has different cognitive abilities, the questions in this book are at varied skill levels. The exercises may or may not require a great deal of parental guidance to complete, depending on your child's abilities, prior test prep experience, or prior testing experience. Most sections of the Workbook begin with a relatively easy question. We suggest always completing at least the first question together, ensuring your child is not confused about what the question asks or with the directions.

"BUBBLES" NOTE: Your child will most likely have to fill in "bubbles" (the circles) to indicate answer choices. Show your child how to fill in the bubble to indicate his/her answer choice using a pencil. If your child needs to change his/her answer, (s)he should erase the original mark and fill in the new choice.

SCORING NOTE: Check with your school/program for its scoring procedure and admissions requirements. Here is a general summary of the COGAT® scoring process. First, your child's raw score is established. This is the number of questions correctly answered. Points are not deducted for questions answered incorrectly. Next, this score is compared to other test-takers of his/her same age group (and, for the COGAT®, the same grade level) using various indices to then calculate your child's stanine (a score from one to nine) and percentile rank. If your child achieved the percentile rank of 98%, then (s)he scored as well as or better than 98% of test-takers. In general, gifted programs accept scores of *at least* 98% or *higher*. Please note that a percentile rank "score" cannot be obtained from our practice material. This material has not been given to a large enough sample of test-takers to develop any kind of base score necessary for percentile rank calculations.

QUESTION EXAMPLES & EXPLANATIONS This section introduces the nine COGAT® question types with simple examples/explanations. Questions in Practice Test 1 & 2 will be more challenging than those below.

VERBAL BATTERY

1. VERBAL ANALOGIES

Directions: Look at the first set of words. Try to figure out how they belong together. Next, look at the second set of words. The answer is missing. Figure out which answer choice would make the second set go together in the same way that the first set goes together.

toe > foot : petal > ? stem bee leg flower colorful

Explanation Here are some strategies to help your child select the correct answer:

- Try to come up with a "rule" describing how the first set goes together. Take this rule, apply it to the first word in the second set. Determine which answer choice makes the second set follow the same "rule." If more than one choice works, you need a more specific rule. Here, a "rule" for the first set is that "the first word (toe) is part of the second word (foot)." In the next set, using this rule, "flower" is the answer. A petal is part of a flower.
- Another strategy is to come up with a sentence describing how the first set of words go together. A sentence would be: A toe is part of a foot. Then, take this sentence and apply it to the word in the second set: A petal is part of a ?. Figure out which answer choice would best complete the sentence. (It would be "flower.")
- Ensure your child does not choose a word simply because it *has to do with* the first set. For example, choice A ("stem") *has to do with* a petal, but does not follow the rule.

The simple examples will introduce your child to analogical thinking. Read the "Question" then "Answer Choices" to your child. Which choice goes best? (The answer is underlined.)

Analogy Logic	Question	Answer Choices (Answer is Underlined)			
• Antonyms	On *is to* Off -as- Hot *is to* ?	Warm	Sun	Cold	Oven
• Synonyms	Big *is to* Large -as- Horrible *is to* ?	Tired	Stale	Sour	Awful
• Whole: Part	Tree *is to* Branch -as- House *is to* ?	Street	Apartment	Room	Home
• Degree	Good *is to* Excellent -as- Tired *is to* ?	Boring	Exhausted	Drowsy	Slow
• Object: Location	Sun *is to* Sky -as- Swing *is to* ?	Playground	Monkey Bars	Sidewalk	Grass
• Same Animal Class	Turkey *is to* Parrot -as- Ant *is to* ?	Worm	Beetle	Duck	Spider
• Object: Creator	Painting *is to* Artist -as- Furniture *is to* ?	Carpenter	Tool	Chair	Potter
• Object: Container	Ice Cube *is to* Ice Tray -as- Flower *is to* ?	Petal	Vase	Smell	Florist
• Tool: Worker	Paintbrush *is to* Artist -as- Microscope *is to* ?	Telescope	Scientist	Lab	Fireman
• Object: 3D Shape	Ball *is to* Sphere -as- Dice *is to* ?	Line	Square	Cone	Cube
• Object: Location Used	Jet *is to* Sky -as- Canoe *is to* ?	Boat	Paddle	Water	Sail
• Object: Location Used	Chalk *is to* Chalkboard -as- Paintbrush *is to* ?	Artist	Easel	Paint	Eraser

2. VERBAL CLASSIFICATION

Directions: Look at the three words on the top row. Figure out how the words are alike. Next, look at the words in the answer choices. Which word goes best with the three words in the top row?

cake bread muffin

A. bakery B. sherbet C. cookie D. syrup E. sugar

Explanation Come up with a "rule" describing how they're alike. Then, see which answer choice follows the rule. If more than one choice does, you need a more specific rule.

- At first, test-takers may say the rule for the top words is that "they are all a kind of food." However, more than one answer choice would fit this rule. A more specific rule is needed. A more specific rule would be that "the foods are baked foods." Therefore, the best answer is "cookie."
- Ensure your child does not choose a word simply because it has to do with the top three. For example, choice A (bakery) has to do with the three, as all three could be found at a bakery. However, "bakery" is not a baked food.

Another simple example:

fall spring summer

A. warm B. season C. month D. winter E. weather

This example demonstrates a common mistake. Note answer choice "B", season. Here, the question logic (or, rule) is "seasons." A child, having the rule "seasons" in their mind, may mistakenly choose "season." However, the answer is "winter," because "winter," like the top three words, is an *example* of a season.

Below are additional simple examples to introduce your child to classification logic.

• function and uses of common objects (i.e., writing and drawing / measuring / cutting / drinking / eating)
Fork / Chopsticks / Knife — Choices: Stove / Straw / Meat / Spoon — (Used For Eating)

• location of common objects
Refrigerator / Cabinet / Table — Choices: Bed / Restaurant / Oven / Shower — (Found In Kitchens)

• appearance of common objects (i.e., color; objects in pairs; objects with stripes vs. spots; object's shape)
Ketchup / Blood / Firetruck — Choices: Cherry / Mustard / Cucumber / Police car — (Red)

• characteristics of common objects (i.e., hot, cold)
Ice / Igloo / Popsicle — Choices: Cookie / Snowman / Palm Tree / Coffee — (Cold)

• animal types
Leopard / Cheetah / Kitten — Choices: Elephant / Giraffe/ Tiger / Bat — (Cats)

• natural habitats
Swamp / River / Pond — Choices: Desert / Mountain / House / Ocean — (Water)

• food growing location (i.e., on a tree, under the ground as a root, or on a vine)
Potato / Carrot / Onion — Choices: Radish / Melon / Pepper / Broccoli — (Root Vegetables)

• professions, community helpers
Doctor / Fireman / Vet — Choices: Witch / Wizard / Teacher / Baby — (Community Helpers)

• clothing (i.e., in what weather it's worn; on what body part it's worn)
Crown / Cowboy Hat / Cap — Choices: Necklace / Helmet / Gloves / Ring — (Worn On Head)

• transportation (i.e., where things travel, land/water/air; do they have wheels?)
Cruise Ship / Yacht / Kayak — Choices: Canoe / Port / Dock / Jeep — (Travel On Water)

3. SENTENCE COMPLETION Directions: First, read the sentence. There is a missing word. Which answer choice goes best in the sentence? (Read the sentences and choices to your child. They may read along silently.)

If you aren't __________ with the vase, it will break.

A. careless B. careful C. clear D. risky E. sloppy

Explanation Here, your child must use the information in the sentence and make inferences (i.e., make a best guess based on the information) and select the best answer choice to fill in the blank. Be sure your child:

• pays attention to each word in the sentence and to each answer choice
• after making his/her choice, (s)he re-reads the complete sentence to ensure the choice makes the *most* sense compared to the other choices (the answer is B)

NON-VERBAL BATTERY

4. FIGURE ANALOGIES Directions: Look at the top set of pictures. They go together in some way. Look at the bottom set. The answer is missing. Figure out which answer choice would make the bottom set go together in the same way that the top set goes together.

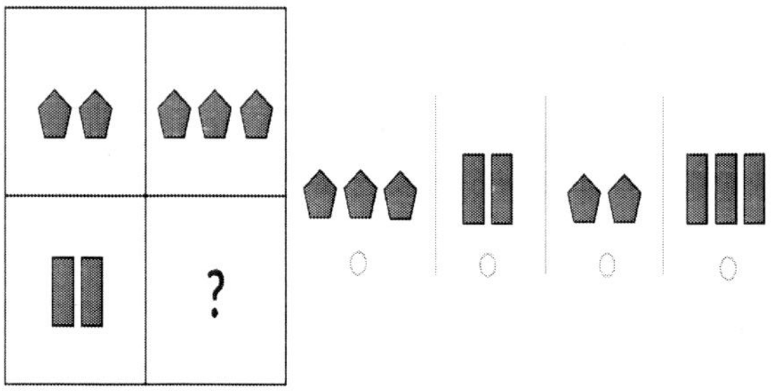

Explanation Come up with a "rule" describing how the top set is related. This "rule" shows how the figures in the left box "change" into the figures in the right box. On the left are 2 pentagons. On the right are 3 pentagons. The rule/change is that one more of the same kind of shape is added. On the bottom are 2 rectangles. The first choice is incorrect, it shows 3 pentagons (not the same shape). The second choice is incorrect (it only shows 2 rectangles). The third choice is incorrect - it has 2 pentagons. The last choice is correct. It has one more of the same shapes from the left box.

Here is a list of basic Figure Analogy "changes." (Test questions include this logic, but questions are more challenging.)

1. Color

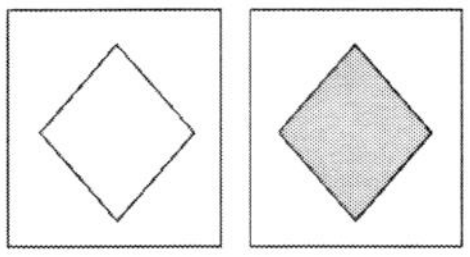

2. Size

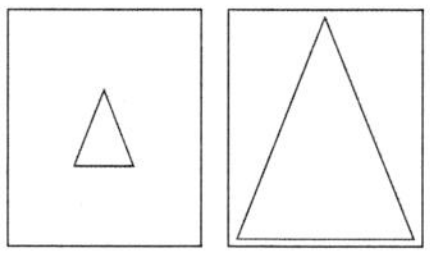

3. Amount

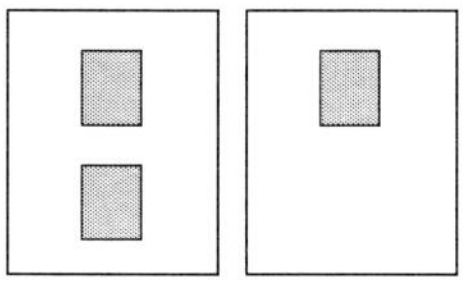

4. Color Reversal

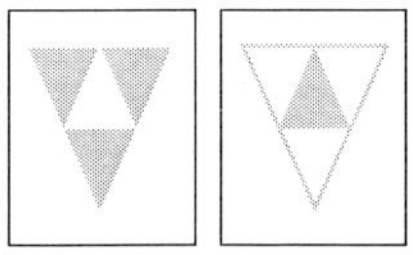

5. Whole: Part

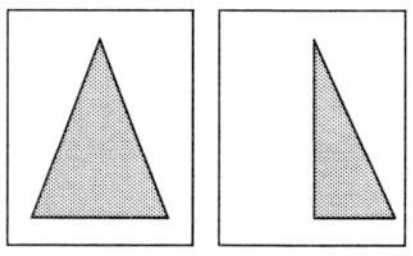

6. Number of Shape Sides

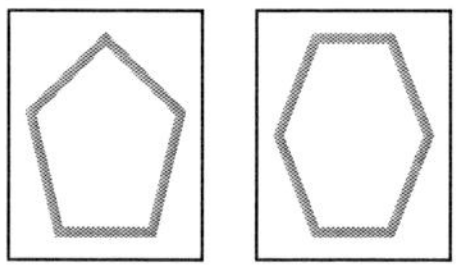

7. Rotation: 90° clock-wise

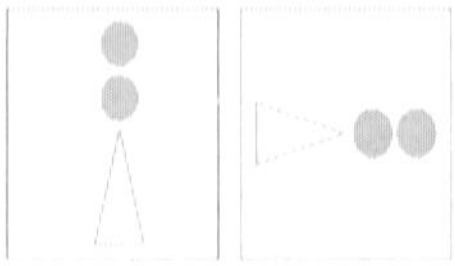

8. Rotation: 90° counter-clockwise

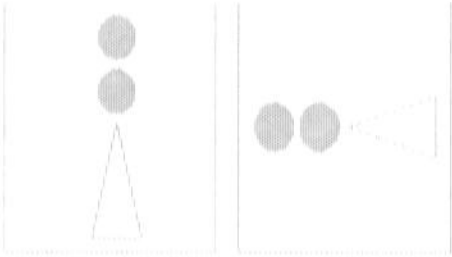

9. Line Direction

10. Flip / Mirror Image

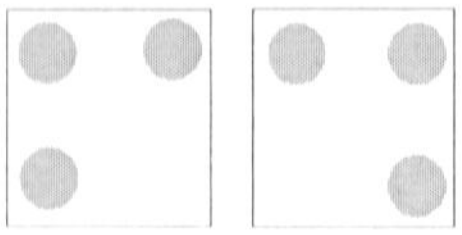

11. Two Changes: Rotation & Quantity

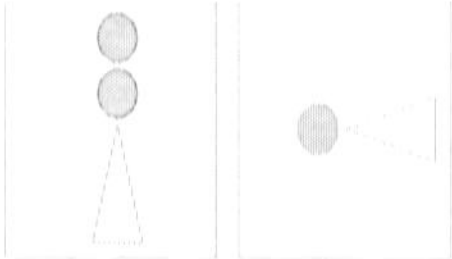

12. Two Changes: Rotation & Color

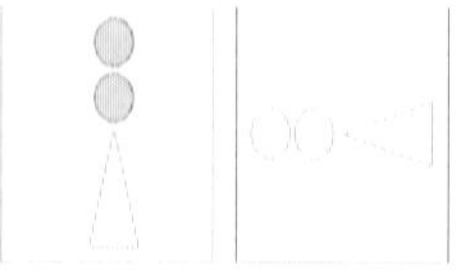

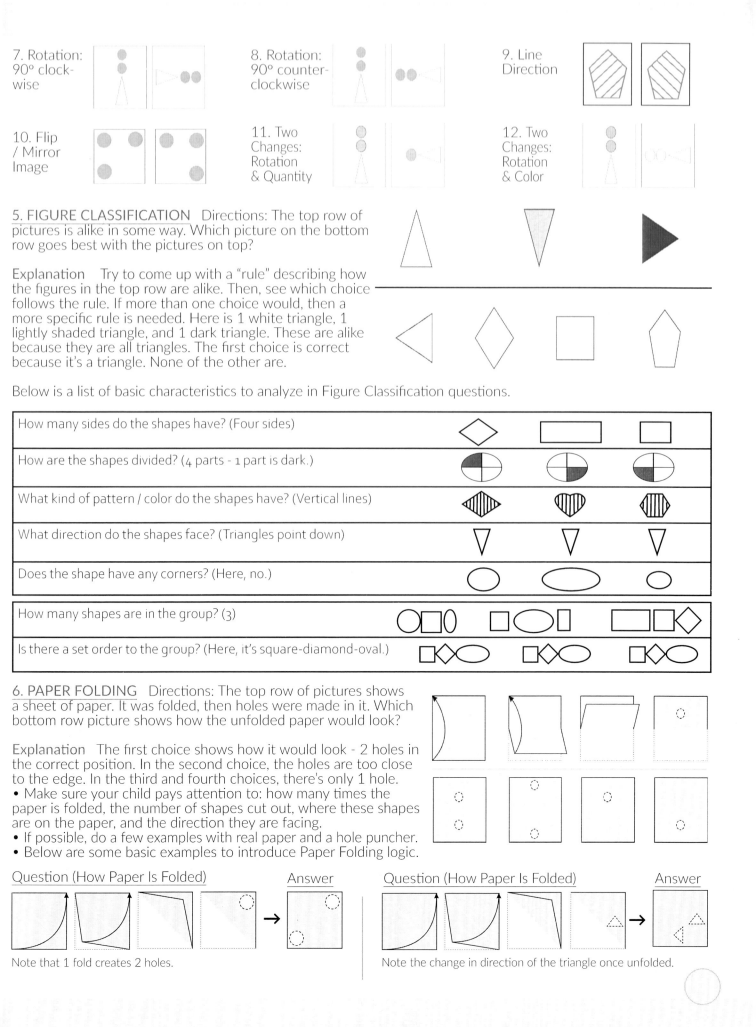

5. FIGURE CLASSIFICATION Directions: The top row of pictures is alike in some way. Which picture on the bottom row goes best with the pictures on top?

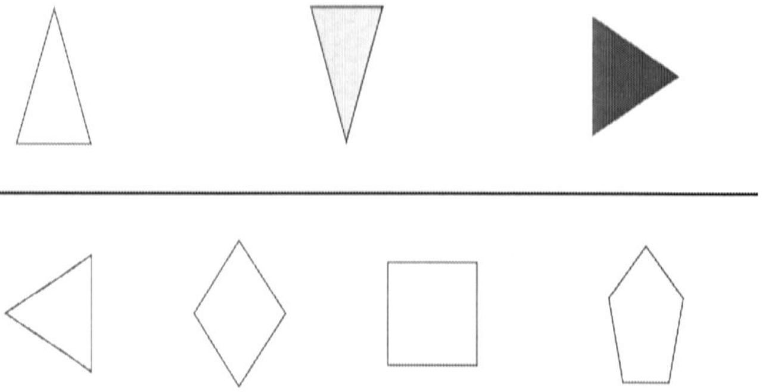

Explanation Try to come up with a "rule" describing how the figures in the top row are alike. Then, see which choice follows the rule. If more than one choice would, then a more specific rule is needed. Here is 1 white triangle, 1 lightly shaded triangle, and 1 dark triangle. These are alike because they are all triangles. The first choice is correct because it's a triangle. None of the other are.

Below is a list of basic characteristics to analyze in Figure Classification questions.

How many sides do the shapes have? (Four sides)	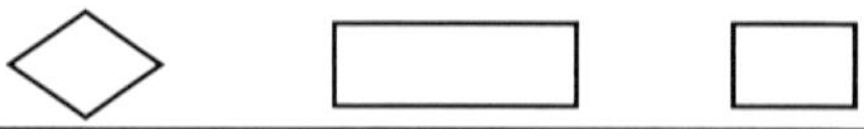
How are the shapes divided? (4 parts - 1 part is dark.)	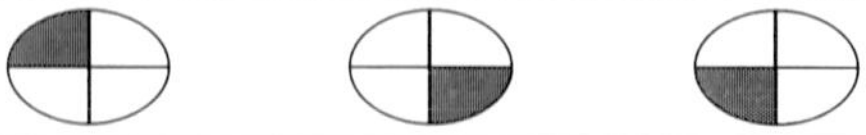
What kind of pattern / color do the shapes have? (Vertical lines)	
What direction do the shapes face? (Triangles point down)	
Does the shape have any corners? (Here, no.)	
How many shapes are in the group? (3)	
Is there a set order to the group? (Here, it's square-diamond-oval.)	

6. PAPER FOLDING Directions: The top row of pictures shows a sheet of paper. It was folded, then holes were made in it. Which bottom row picture shows how the unfolded paper would look?

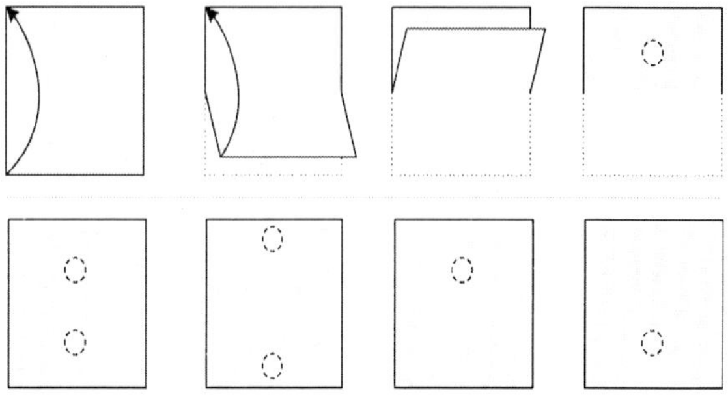

Explanation The first choice shows how it would look - 2 holes in the correct position. In the second choice, the holes are too close to the edge. In the third and fourth choices, there's only 1 hole.

• Make sure your child pays attention to: how many times the paper is folded, the number of shapes cut out, where these shapes are on the paper, and the direction they are facing.
• If possible, do a few examples with real paper and a hole puncher.
• Below are some basic examples to introduce Paper Folding logic.

Question (How Paper Is Folded) Answer

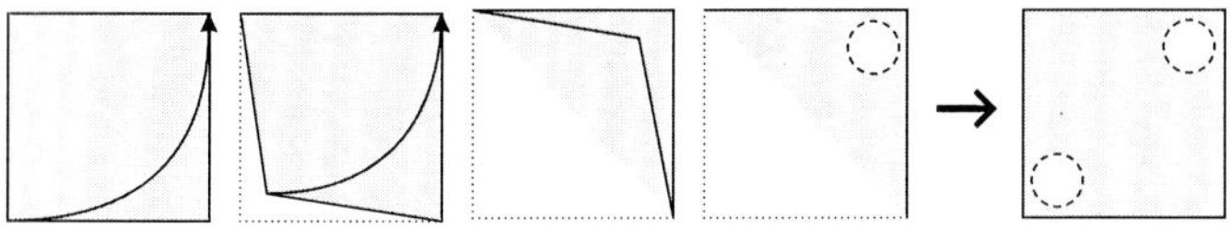

Note that 1 fold creates 2 holes.

Question (How Paper Is Folded) Answer

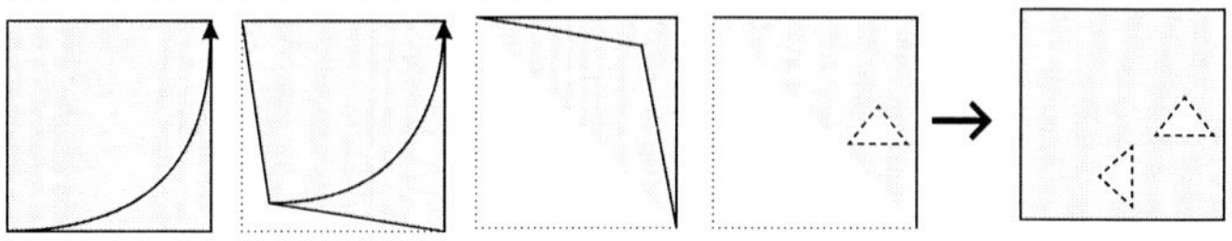

Note the change in direction of the triangle once unfolded.

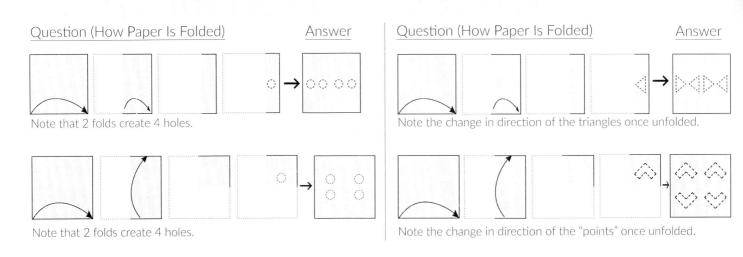

Question (How Paper Is Folded) | Answer

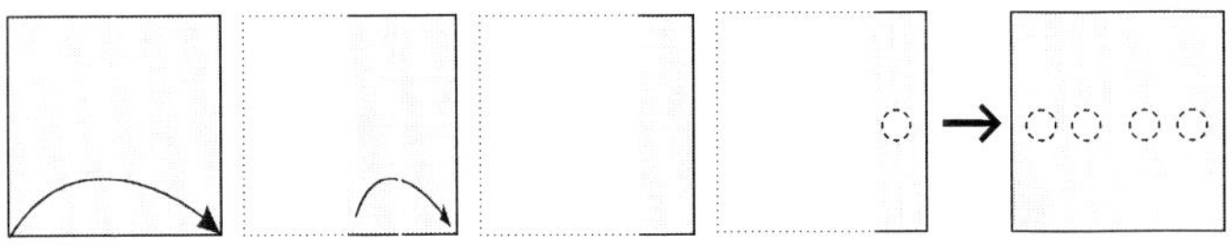

Note that 2 folds create 4 holes.

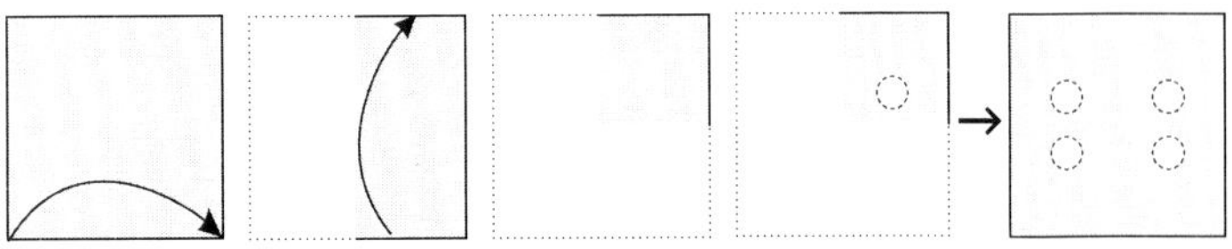

Note that 2 folds create 4 holes.

Question (How Paper Is Folded) | Answer

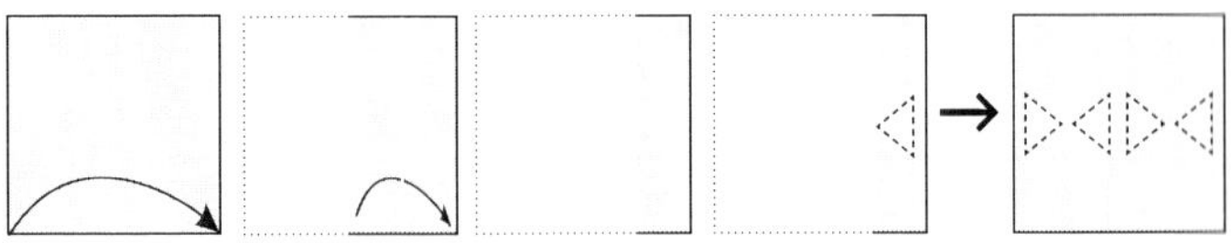

Note the change in direction of the triangles once unfolded.

Note the change in direction of the "points" once unfolded.

QUANTITATIVE BATTERY

7. NUMBER PUZZLES Directions: What answer choice should you put in the place of the question mark so that both sides of the equal sign total the same amount?

Explanation These questions have two formats. The first example is a fairly standard math problem and self-explanatory. In the second example, your child should first replace the black shape with its number value. If your child gets stumped on any Number Puzzles, (s)he can always test out each answer to find the one that works.

1.	10 = 25 - ?	A. 25	B. 15	C. 20	D. 5	E. 0
2.	? = ◆ + 2	A. 1	B. 2	C. 3	D. 0	E. 4
	◆ = 1					

8. NUMBER SERIES Directions: Which answer choice would complete the pattern?

15	13	11	9	7	?
A.1	B.3	C.5	D.6	E.4	

Explanation The numbers have made a pattern. To help your child figure out the pattern, have them write the difference between each number and the next. In this basic example, the pattern is: -2. In easier questions, the difference between all consecutive numbers is the same (i.e., the difference between 15 & 13 = 2 and between 13 & 11 = 2). However, sometimes the difference will not continuously repeat itself, as in these examples:

9	8	6	5	3	2	?	The pattern is: -1, -2, -1, -2, etc. & the answer is 0.
1	2	4	7	11	16	?	The pattern is: +1, +2, +3, +4, etc. & the answer is 22.
4	5	9	4	5	9	?	The pattern is: 4-5-9 & the answer is 4.

9. NUMBER ANALOGIES Directions: Look at the first two sets of numbers. Come up with a rule that both of these sets follow. Take this rule to figure out which answer choice goes in the place of the question mark.

[10 → 5] [8 → 4] [14 → ?] A. 2 B. 7 C. 28 D. 16 E. 1

Explanation Come up with a rule to explain how the first number "changes" into the second. It could use addition, subtraction, multiplication, or division. Have your child write the rule by *each* pair. Make sure it works with *both* pairs. The rule is "÷ by 2", so 7 is the answer.

TEST-TAKING TIPS

COGAT® Checklist (tips for answering questions)

✓ **#1: Do not rush.** Look carefully at the question and each answer choice.
✓ **#2: Use process of elimination.** You receive points for the number of correct answers. You will not lose points for incorrect answers. Instead of leaving a question unanswered, at least guess. First, eliminate any answers that are obviously not correct. Then, guess from those remaining.
✓ **#3: Double check.** Before marking your answer, double check it by going through the question and answer to make sure it makes sense. "Talking" silently to yourself as you go through it is a good idea.
✓ **#4: Be sure to choose only ONE answer.** When you fill in your bubble sheet, fill in only ONE bubble per question - instead of making a careless mistake and filling in two.

- Be sure to read the first section at the beginning of each group of questions in Practice Test 1. These have even more tips specific for each question type. They also have reminders to follow the "COGAT® Checklist" above.

Common Sense Tips

- **Get enough sleep.** This one is so obvious, yet so important. Studies have shown a link between not getting enough sleep and lower test scores.
- **Eat a breakfast for sustained energy and concentration.** (complex carbohydrates and protein; avoid foods/drinks high in sugar)
- **Use the restroom prior to the test.** The administrator may not allow a break during the test.
- **Don't get overly stressed.** Try not to worry about preparing for the test or the test itself. Instead, focus on doing your best. The test will have challenging questions, and sometimes, you will simply not know the answer. When this happens, instead of worrying, remain focused on answering the question the best you can and using the process of elimination (outlined above).

VERBAL ANALOGIES

Directions: Look at the first set of words. They go together in some way. Next, look at the second set. Then, look at the answer choices. Which answer choice goes with the word in the second set in the same way that the first set of words goes together?

Notes: Analogies compare sets of items, and the way they are related can easily be missed. Work through these together to figure out how the first set is related. Here are two strategies.

Strategy 1: Come up with a "rule" to describe how the first set is related. Then, take this "rule," use it together with the second set and figure out which of the answer choices would follow that same rule. For answer choices that do not follow it, eliminate them. If more than one choice would follow it, then come up with a rule that is more specific.

Strategy 2: Think of a sentence that describes how the first set is related. Then, complete the same process you completed with the "rule". Apply the sentence to the answer choices. Eliminate those that do not work with the sentence. If more than one choice would work, then come up with a sentence that is more specific.

With both strategies, you may need to try a different rule / sentence if your first one does not work. (See example below.) Also, make sure to go through the checklist at the top of page 9.

Example (#1): How do "parrot" and "feathers" go together? What "rule" or sentence could describe how they go together? *Rule: The first object (parrot) uses the second object (feathers) to help it fly. Sentence: A parrot uses its feathers to help it fly.* However, look at the second set and the answer choices. A goldfish does not fly. We need to try a different rule/sentence. *Rule: The first object (parrot) is covered with many of the second object (feathers). Sentence: A parrot is covered with many feathers.* Look at the word "goldfish". Which of the choices follow this rule? Scales (choice E).

1 **parrot → feathers : goldfish → ?**

○ skin ○ water ○ aquarium ○ gills ● scales

2 **circle → sphere : square → ?**

○ rectangle ● cube ○ cylinder ○ cone ○ shape

3 **fashion designer → clothes : architect → ?**

○ carpenter ● buildings ○ welder ○ clothing ○ drawings

4 **Neptune → farthest : Mercury → ?**

○ distance ○ satellite ○ planet ● closest ○ coldest

5 **tall → towering : scary → ?**

- ghostly
- spooky
- daunting
- surprising
- terrifying

6 **temperature → thermometer : distance → ?**

- miles
- meters
- speed
- anemometer
- odometer

7 **performers → trio : wheels → ?**

- triplets
- tricycle
- triangle
- bicycle
- tires

8 **paper → tree : flour → ?**

- leaf
- sugar
- grain
- bread
- root

9 **glass → smooth : pavement → ?**

- black
- road
- cement
- rough
- sharp

10 **casino → gamble : restaurant → ?**

- reserve
- plates
- dine
- chef
- waiter

11 **right → write : cereal → ?**

- ethereal
- clear
- serial
- series
- serious

12 **summary → synopsis : swift → ?**

- rapid
- balanced
- increase
- unstable
- glide

13 **wild → tame : optimistic → ?**

- exhausted
- apologetic
- dramatic
- positive
- pessimistic

14 **goose → waddle : snake → ?**

○ reptile ○ cobra ○ poisonous ○ slither ○ bite

15 **welder → metal : carpenter → ?**

○ walls ○ furniture ○ wood ○ nail ○ saw

16 **fierce → ferocious : old → ?**

○ past ○ ancient ○ time ○ history ○ extinct

17 **helmet → protect : vehicle → ?**

○ transport ○ track ○ truck ○ highway ○ automobile

18 **flee → fled : wind → ?**

○ windy ○ went ○ want ○ blew ○ wound

19 **debate → moderator : game → ?**

○ fan ○ referee ○ announcer ○ player ○ winner

20 **numerical → numbers : chronological → ?**

○ words ○ sort ○ historical ○ times ○ past

21 **teacher → occupation : ferry → ?**

○ sail ○ float ○ passenger ○ canoe ○ vessel

22 **story → novel : run → ?**

○ exercise ○ sprint ○ marathon ○ track ○ lap

VERBAL CLASSIFICATION

Directions: Look at the three words on the top row. Figure out how the words are alike. Next, look at the words in the row of answer choices. Which word goes best with the three words in the top row?

Parent note: As you did with Verbal Analogies questions, together, try to come up with a "rule" to describe how the top three words are alike and go together. Then, take this "rule," and figure out which of the answer choices would best follow that same rule. If none of the choices work, you need to try a different rule. If more than one choice would work, then come up with a rule that is more specific. (See example below.)

Also, make sure to go through the checklist at the top of page 9.

Example (#1): How do the words "sea", "gulf", and "lagoon" go together? What is a rule that describes how they go together?

These all contain water. This would be a good "rule", however, a marsh, fountain, and aqueduct (and a ditch, when it rains) could all contain water. We need a more specific rule.

These are all bodies of water. (Also, they are not man-made. Each is naturally occurring. However, the "bodies of water" rule is sufficient.) The answer would be choice D, marsh.

1 **sea** **gulf** **lagoon**

○ rain ○ ditch ○ aqueduct ● marsh ○ fountain

2 **theatre** **auditorium** **stadium**

○ event ○ skyscraper ● arena ○ concert ○ lawn

3 **second** **gram** **foot**

○ stopwatch ○ size ○ decimal ● liter ○ tape measure

4 **rapid** **prompt** **brisk**

○ lagging ● swift ○ trip ○ flight ○ speed

5	**Mars**	**Earth**	**Uranus**		
	○ Venus	○ planet	○ Orion	○ asteroid	○ Galileo
6	**budget**	**calculate**	**currency**		
	○ sync	○ speedometer	○ magnify	○ coupon	○ gallon
7	**drawer**	**chest**	**crate**		
	○ hanger	○ cushion	○ chair	○ barrel	○ clip
8	**median**	**midst**	**midpoint**		
	○ pair	○ double	○ part	○ section	○ center
9	**clever**	**smart**	**bright**		
	○ rapid	○ intelligent	○ ignorant	○ memorable	○ detailed
10	**semester**	**decade**	**year**		
	○ day	○ first	○ last	○ calendar	○ clock
11	**toaster**	**microwave**	**stove**		
	○ match	○ iron	○ appliance	○ refrigerator	○ blender
12	**Spain**	**Japan**	**Kenya**		
	○ Asia	○ Arctic	○ Argentina	○ Alaska	○ country
13	**grapes**	**tomatoes**	**melons**		
	○ carrots	○ onions	○ potatoes	○ radishes	○ berries

14 **safe** **vault** **padlock**

- ○ satellite ● shield ○ metal ○ report ○ uniform

15 **physician** **pharmacist** **therapist**

- ○ hospital ○ medical ○ employer ● surgeon ○ electrician

16 **peninsula** **dune** **delta**

- ○ buoy ○ bay ● island ○ tidal ○ ocean

17 **mayor** **legislator** **governor**

- ○ voter ● president ○ ballot ○ principal ○ advisor

18 **scarce** **lacking** **insufficient**

- ○ decent ○ scary ○ plenty ● inadequate ○ lost

19 **matching** **twin** **identical**

- ○ independent ○ collection ○ category ○ unique ● duplicate

20 **constantly** **seldom** **occasionally**

- ○ direct ○ late ● rarely ○ minute ○ schedule

21 **decrease** **diminish** **contract**

- ○ prejudiced ○ illegal ○ skilled ● reduce ○ thoughtful

22 **divide** **separate** **split**

- ● disconnect ○ inclusive ○ combine ○ finish ○ realize

SENTENCE COMPLETION

Directions: First, read the sentence. There is a missing word. Next, look at the row of answer choices below the sentence. Which word would go best in the sentence?

(Note that in some sentences there is only one word missing, and you only need to choose one word. However, in others there are two words missing, and you must choose two words.)

Notes:

- Make sure to read the entire sentence very carefully. To ensure you have not accidentally skipped words or misread them, we suggest "mouthing" the words to yourself. You may even want to read the sentence twice.

- Eliminate answer choices that are clearly incorrect.

- Before making your final choice, read the entire sentence again using the word(s) of your answer choice. Ask yourself if these word(s) make sense in the sentence. Ask yourself if they are the best choice.

- If you have a sentence that requires two words, make sure both words make sense in the sentence and that they are the best choice.

1 **One of the parts of a pharmacist's job is to ____ patients how to properly take medication.**

○ retrieve ○ extend ○ praise ● advise ○ sponsor

2 **There was a(n) ____ change in temperature this week that caused all the snow to melt extremely fast.**

○ slow ○ mild ○ gradual ● abrupt ○ frigid

3 ✓ When our horses move to a new stable far away, they will ride in a special truck that will ____ them there safely.

    ○ remain   ◉ transfer   ○ approach   ○ prance   ○ increase

4 ✗ To determine the ____ of the fire, the investigators must figure out how it started.

    ○ origin   ◉ form   ○ station   ○ flames   ○ summary

5 ✗ Despite the salesperson claiming that the diamond was ____, I could tell it was fake.

    ○ reduced   ○ polished   ○ genuine   ○ negative   ◉ phony

6 ✓ If you don't want to get thirsty, make sure to drink an ____ amount of water.

    ◉ adequate   ○ unequal   ○ inferior   ○ important   ○ obtuse

7 ✓ We needed to ____ the table quickly to use at the picnic, but the complicated directions made it impossible to do so.

    ○ flatten   ◉ assemble   ○ destroy   ○ sketch   ○ raze

8 ✗ The cookbook was a ____ of recipes from each participant in the cooking contest.

● separation ○ browsing ○ compilation ○ watching ○ graph

9 ✓ Without our large ____ to the school's charity, they would not have the money to build the new theater.

○ banquet ● contribution ○ exchange ○ deduction ○ withdrawal

10 ✗ Five championships are a justification of the coach's superstar ____ .

○ referee ○ disappointment ○ disapproval ○ status ● guide

11 ✓ Despite the obvious similarities in the paintings, if you look very closely you can see the ____ differences.

○ shrill ● subtle ○ rude ○ exhausting ○ massive

12 ✓ The police finally located and _____ the thief resting under a bridge that was _____ as a spot where criminals hide.

○ released, known ○ secured, crafted ○ carried, built ○ congratulated, famed ● captured, notorious

13 **One of the positive _____ of the Internet is our _____ to access information whenever we need it.**

- connections, need
- hazards, requirement
- introductions, barrier
- ideas, restriction
- impacts, ability

14 **People's desire to use less plastic would _____ an increase in the use of plastic _____.**

- cause, amounts
- lead to, materials
- result in, alternatives
- merit, bottles
- produce, particles

15 **To be declared the winner of the game, all three judges must ____ that your answer was the best.**

- disagree
- dispute
- direct
- challenge
- concur

16 **Her new company should be a success - it has the _____ to _____ lots of money.**

- absence, produce
- potential, generate
- possibility, lose
- ability, lose
- shortage, avoid

17 **This _____ of the race _____ a rock-climbing wall and tire swing.**

- distance, requires
- entrance, measures
- participant, includes
- phase, consists of
- champion, qualifies

18 The amount of people in the theatre had reached its ____, so they had to stop selling tickets.

- capacity
- minimum
- display
- audience
- reservation

19 The sensor is so powerful that it can _____ _____ any sound - even the sound of a pin drop.

- hide, barely
- conceal, slightly
- identify, barely
- discover, hardly
- detect, virtually

20 It is impossible to _____ Chicago's problems with our town's because of the contrasting sizes of the city and our small town.

- continue
- conclude
- equate
- dismiss
- generalize

21 Our _____ will use sneaky _____, like spying on us, to try to win the war.

- rival, conflicts
- leader, disputes
- ally, plans
- enemy, battles
- adversary, tactics

22 The beginning of this _____ is _____ ; no one in my family really knows why we started doing this every year.

- event, plain
- tradition, obscure
- custom, transparent
- ceremony, distinct
- celebration, clear

FIGURE CLASSIFICATION

Directions: Look at the three pictures on the top row. Figure out how the pictures are alike. Next, look at the pictures in the row of answer choices. Which picture goes best with the three pictures in the top row?

Parent note: As you did with Verbal Classification questions, together, try to come up with a "rule" to describe how the top pictures are alike and go together. Then, take this "rule," and figure out which of the answer choices would best follow that same rule. If your child finds that more than one choice follows the rule, then (s)he should try to come up with a rule that is more specific.

Common "rules" for the designs in Figure Classification include, but are not limited to: (the # question number provides an example)

- **number of sides** (#1)
- **rotation or direction** (#2, #7)
- **color or design** (#3)
- **quantity** (#8)
- **position** (#10*; *See "multiple elements" note below)
- **size of figure / figure's parts** (#11)
- **rounded vs. angled corners** (#14)
- **figure order** (#19)

* **Note on multiple elements:** Frequently, your "rule" will consist of more than one element, combining (but not limited to) the list above, i.e.,: **position and quantity** (#4), **quantity and type** (#5), **design and type** (#6, #9).

Make sure to read through the Answer Key explanations which include additional examples of "rules"/"changes." Also, make sure to go through the checklist at the top of page 9.

Example (#1): How do these 3 shapes go together? What is a rule that describes how they go together? They do not have the same inside "design" because two of the shapes are dark gray, while one is filled with dark gray lines. They are not pointing the same direction. As far as quantity, there is 1 of each of them. However, each answer choice has 1 shape. We need a rule that's more specific. They all have "angled" corners. However, each answer choice has angled corners. Again, we need a rule that's more specific. Let's count the number of sides. Each shape has 7 sides. Choice E has 7 sides. It is the answer.

1

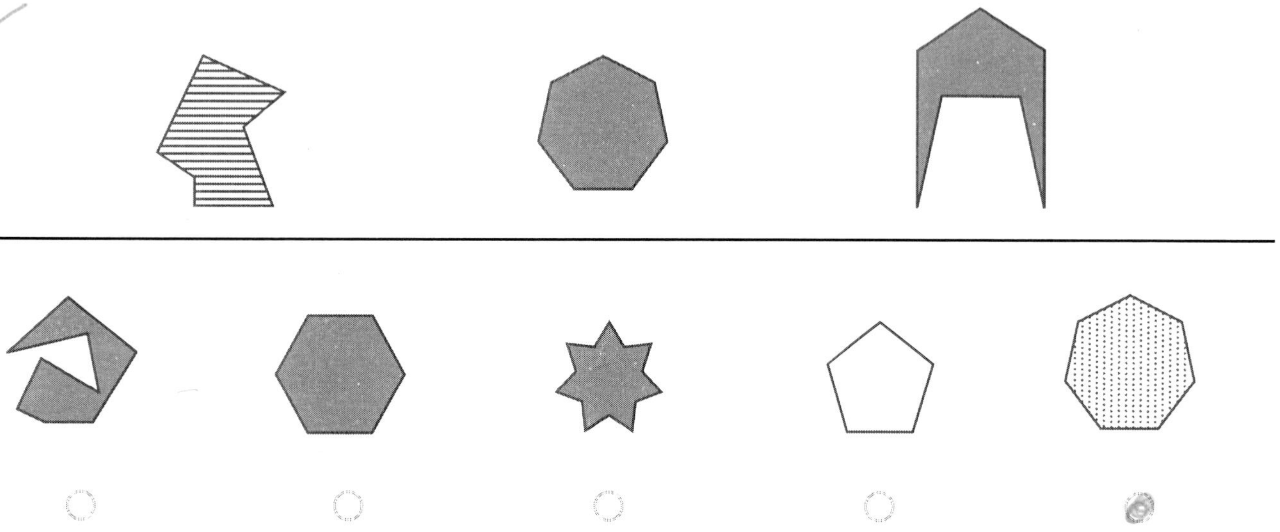

2

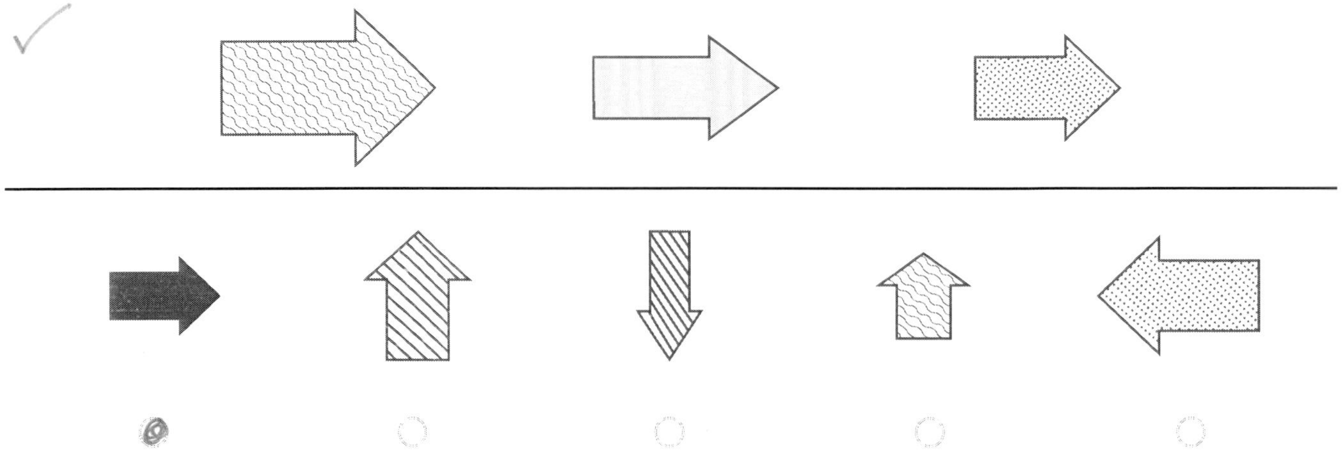

3

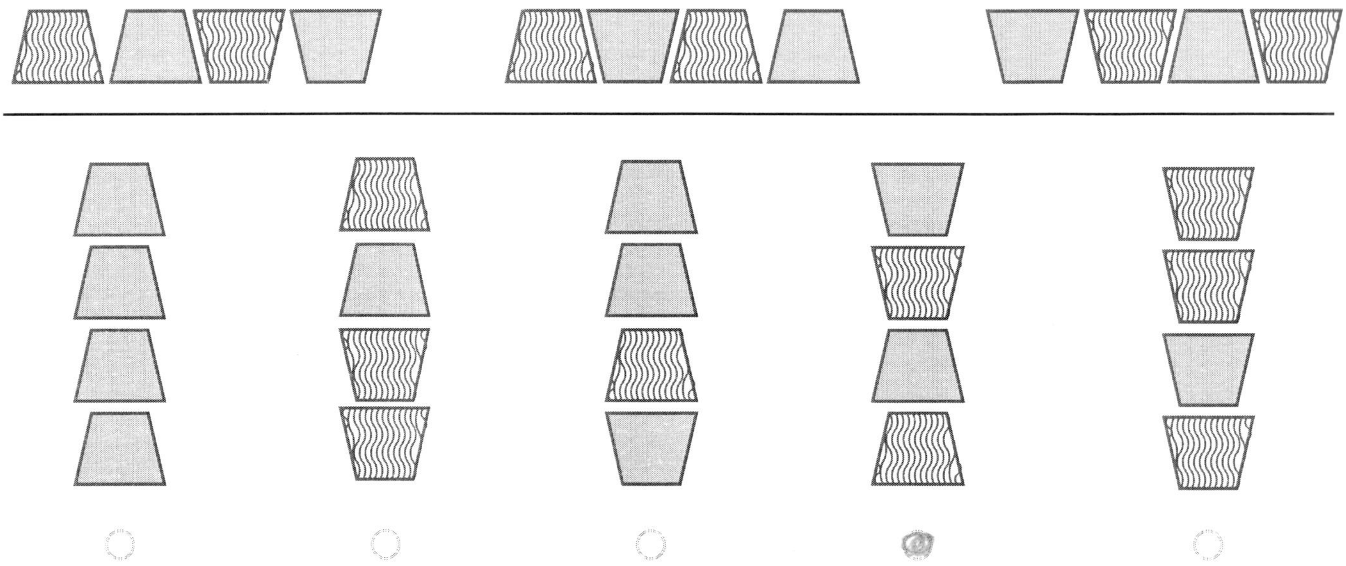

4

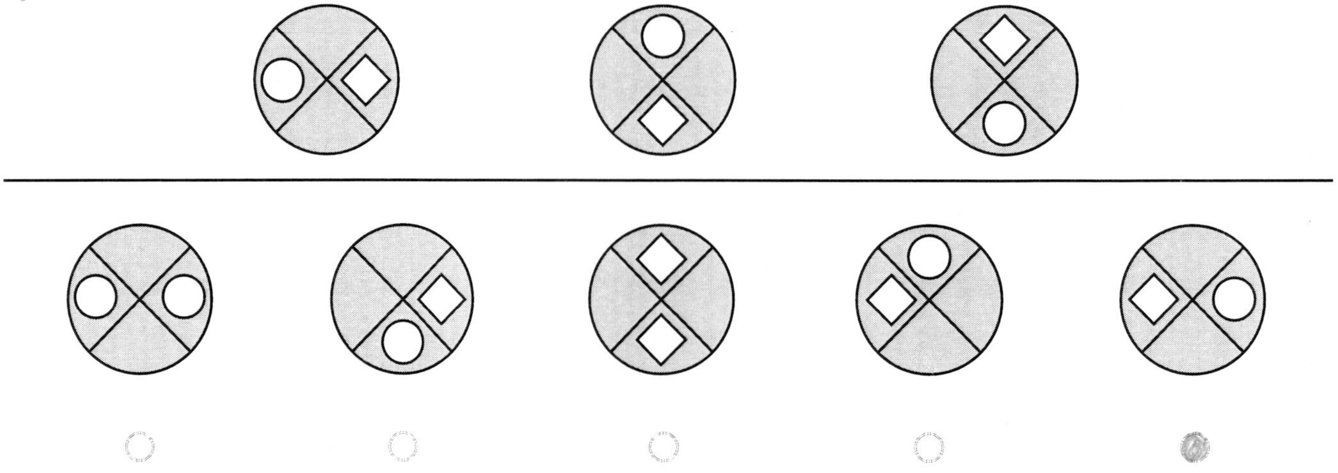

5

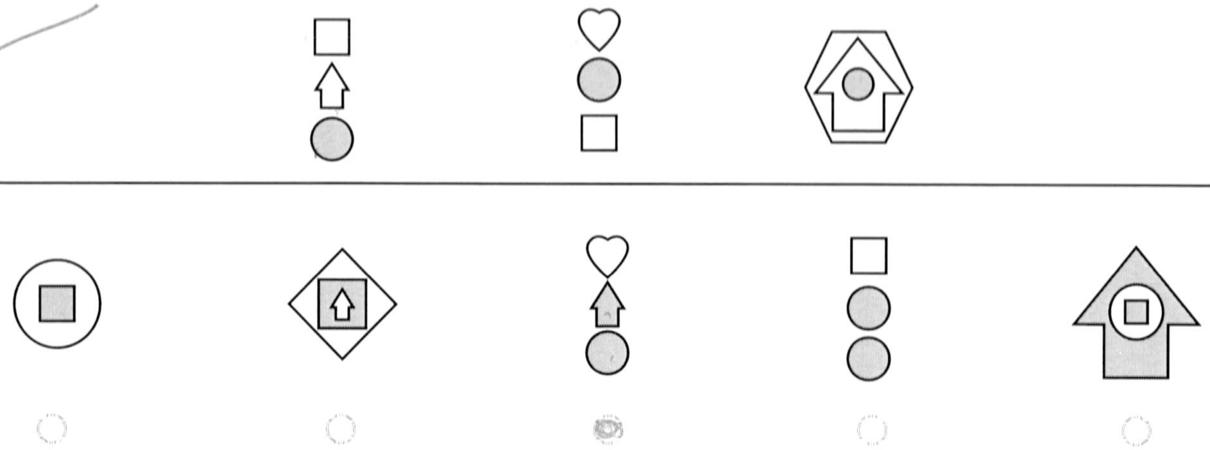

6

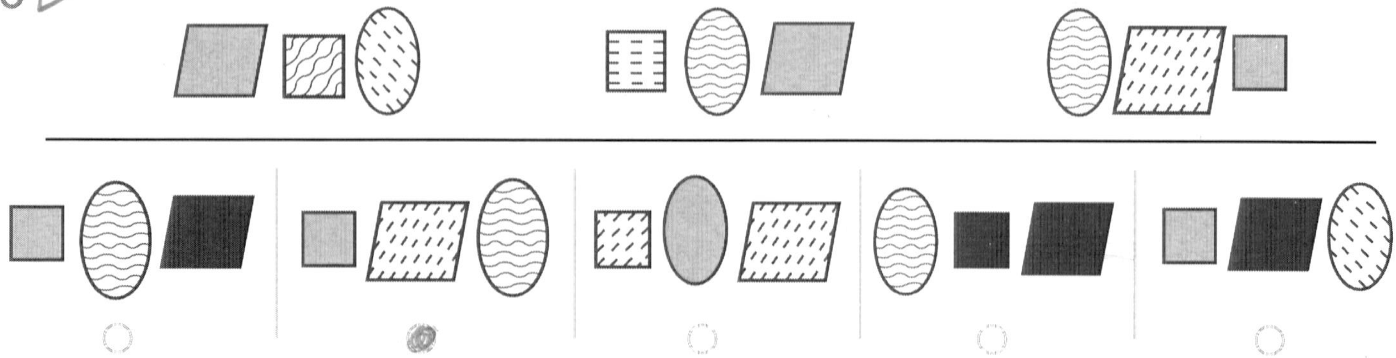

7

8

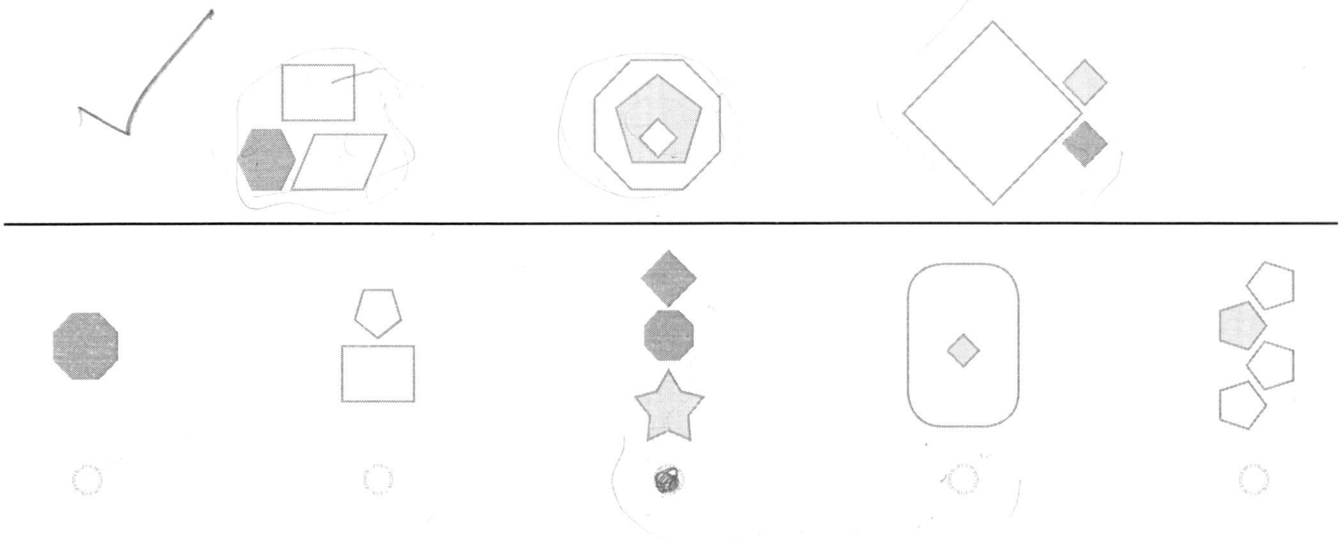

9

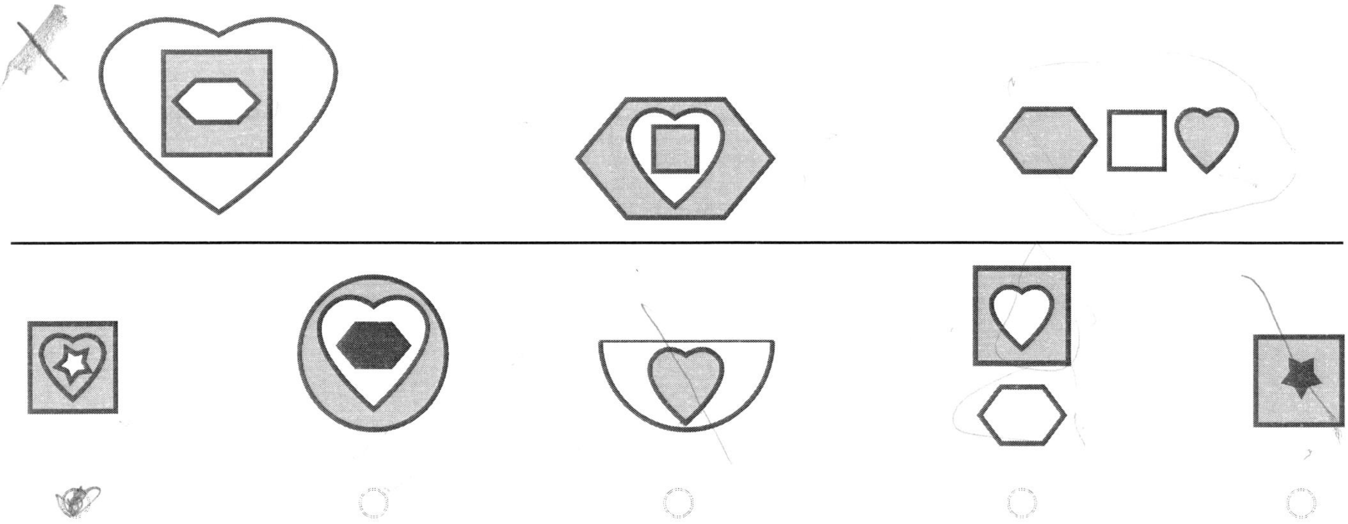

10

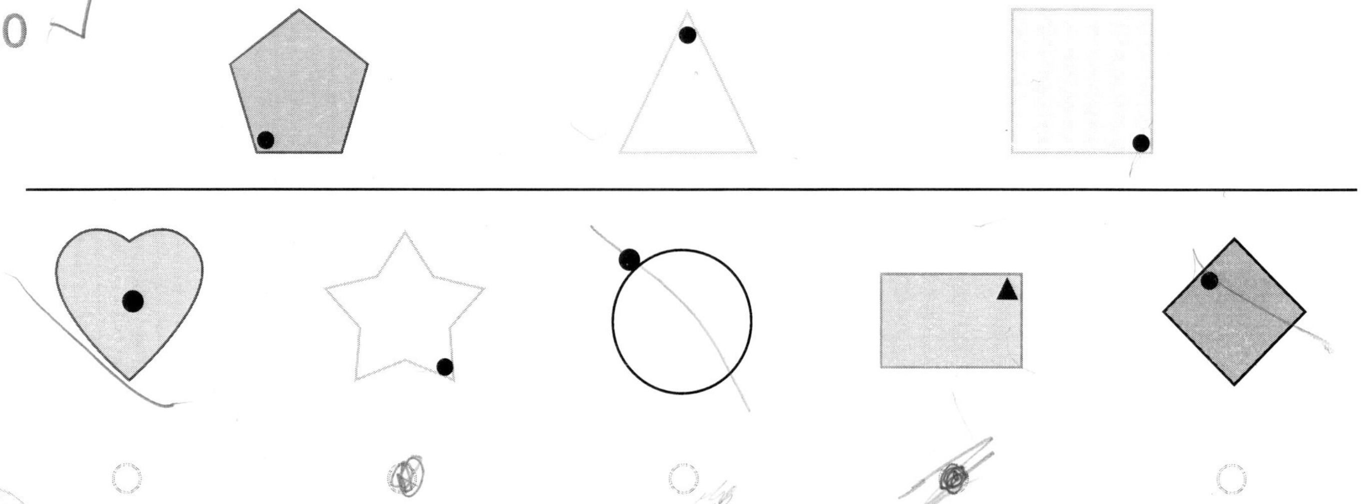

11

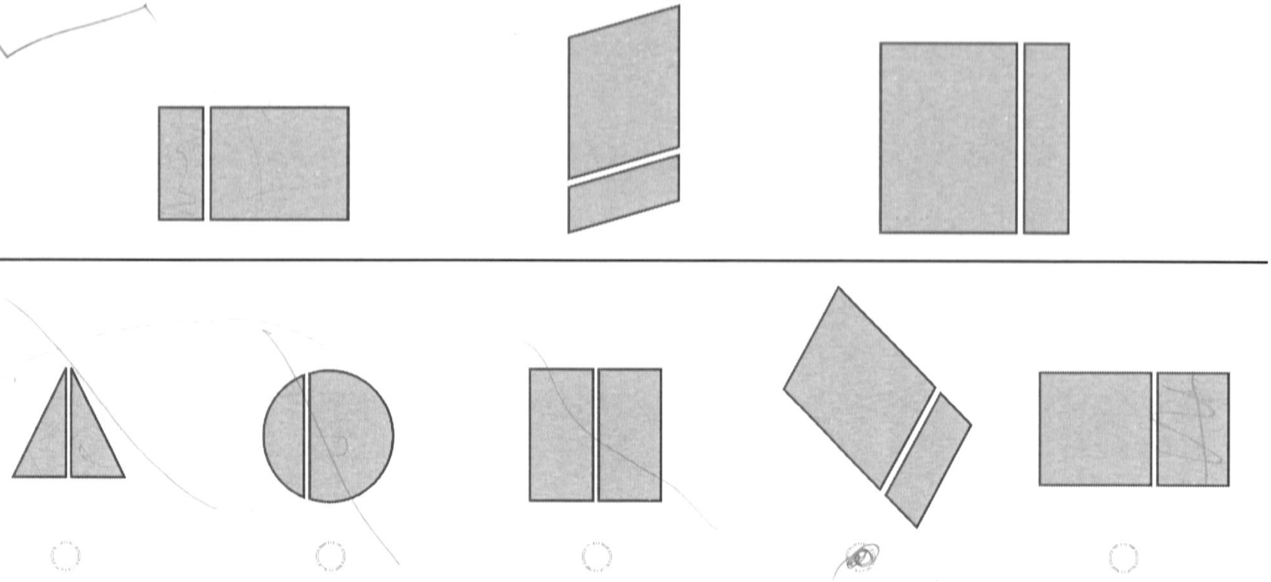

12

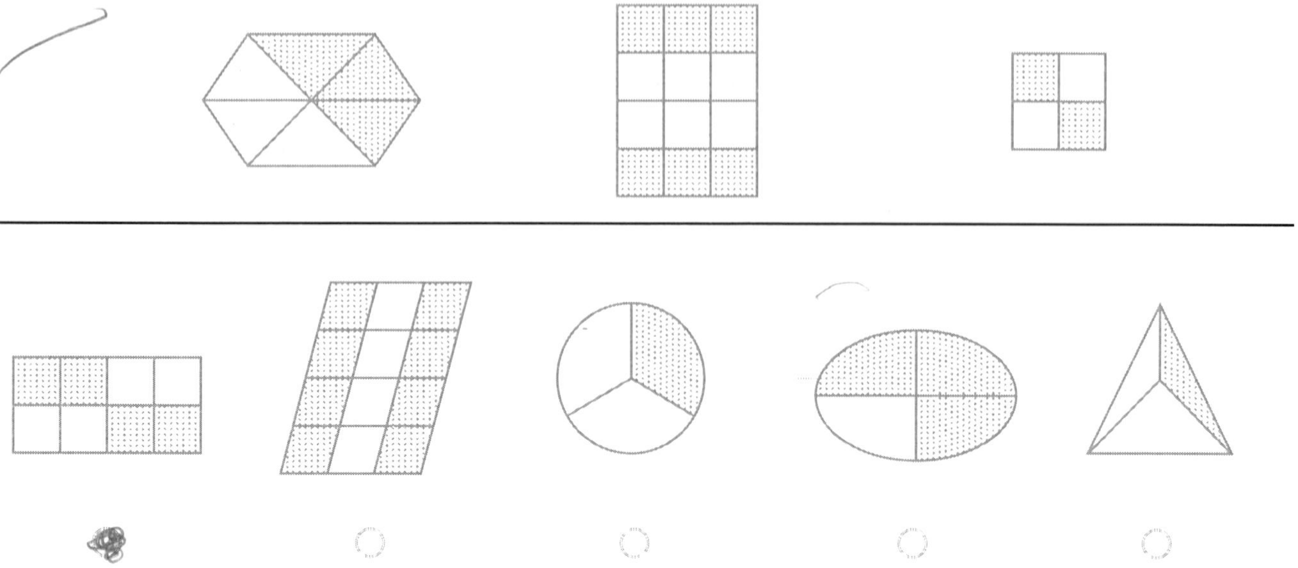

13

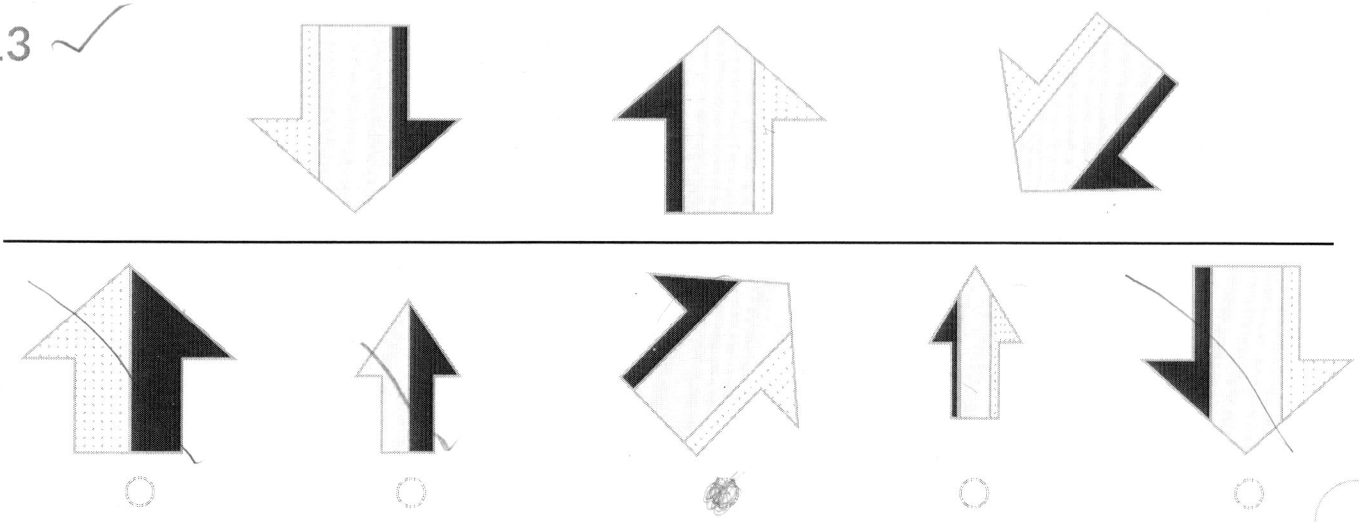

14

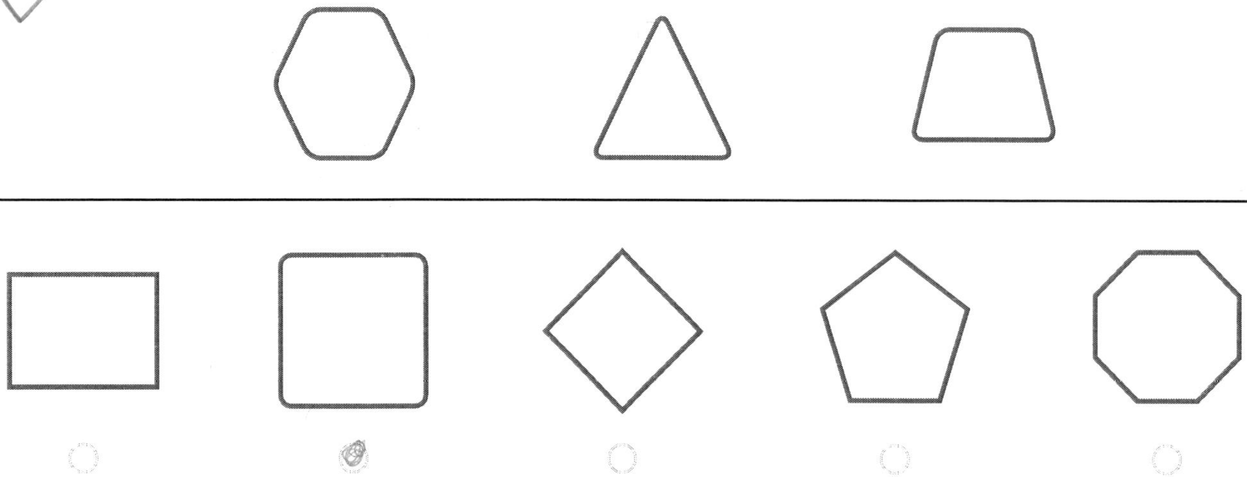

15

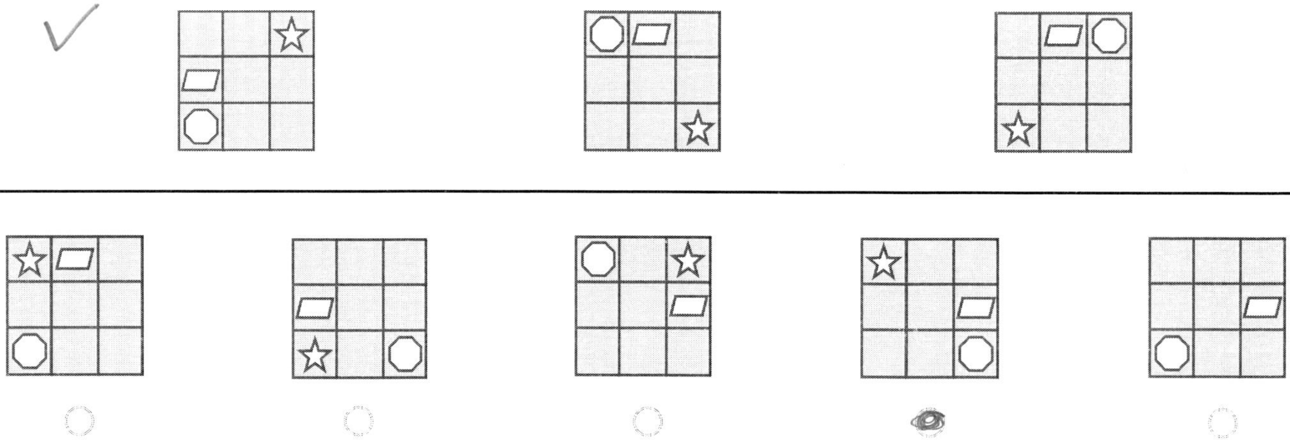

16

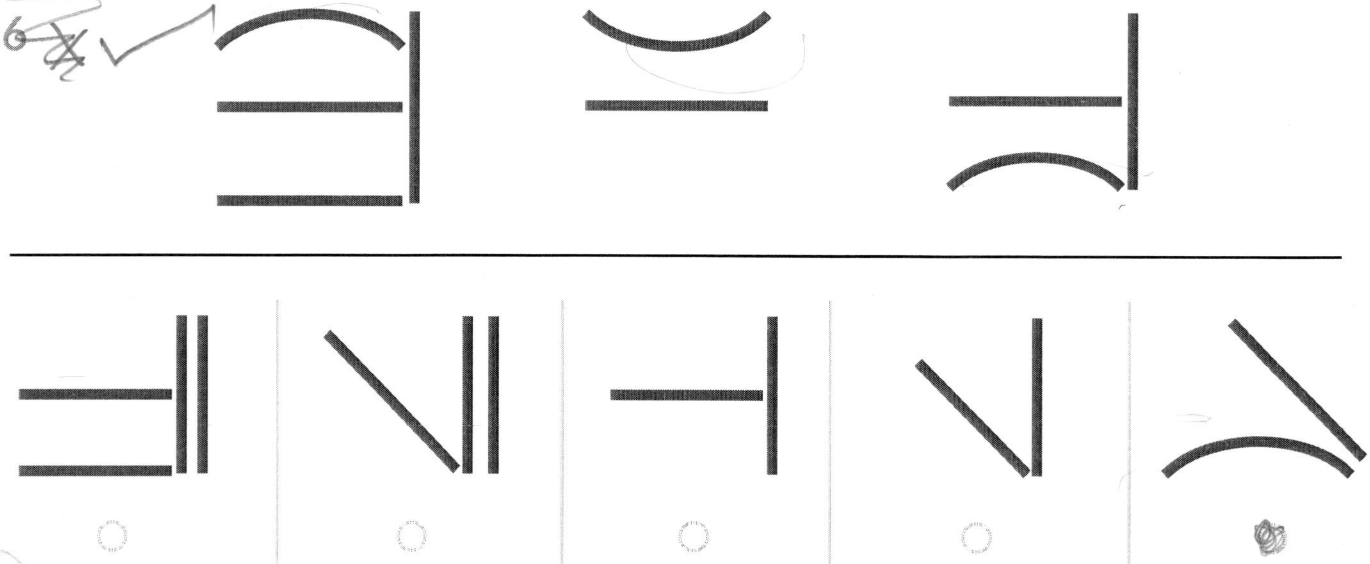

17

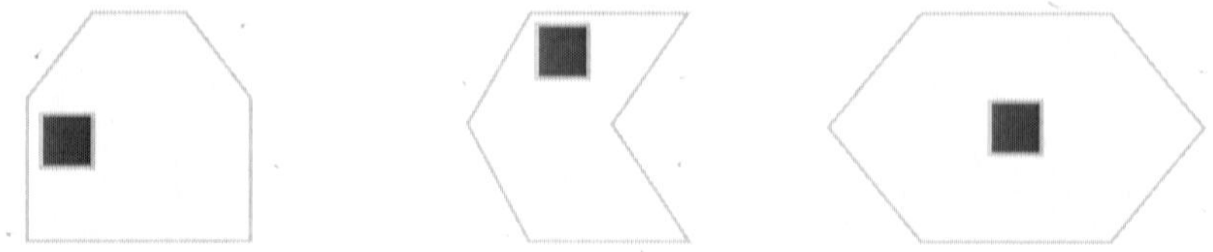

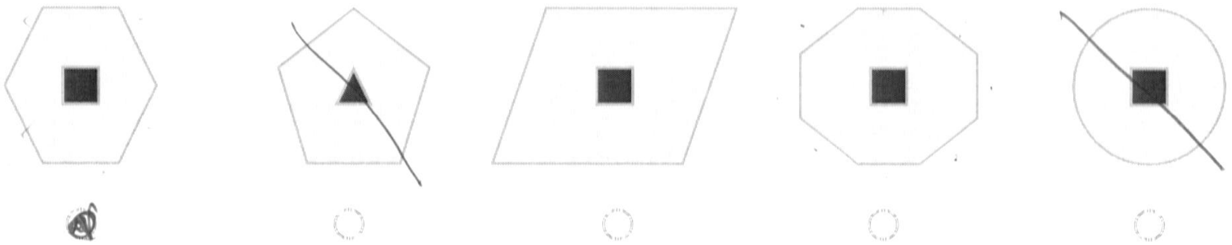

18

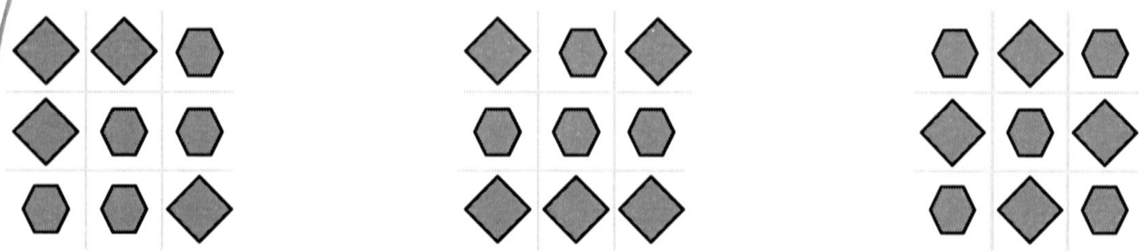

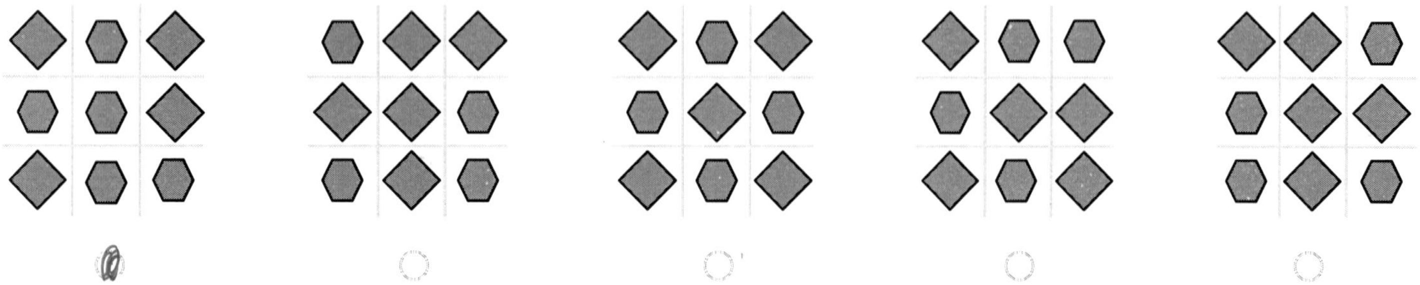

19

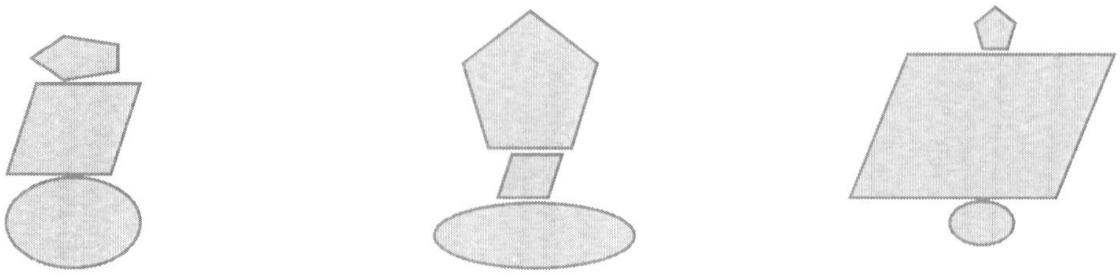

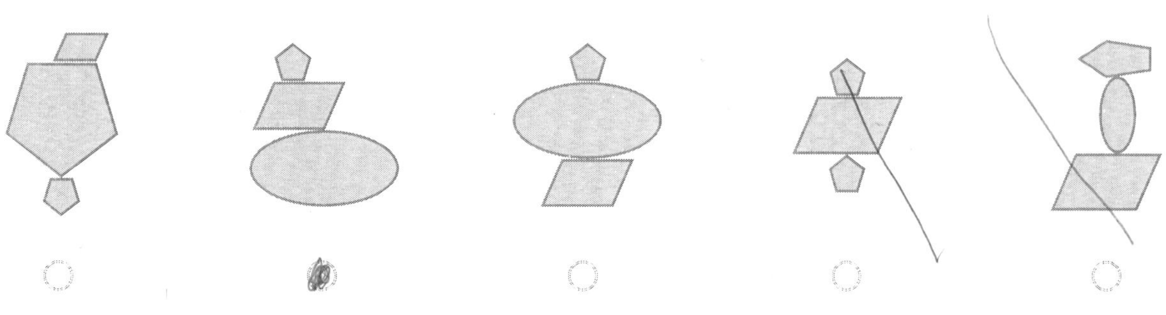

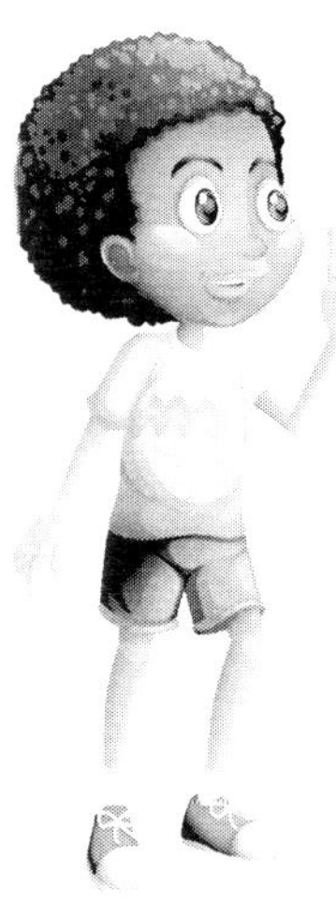

FIGURE ANALOGIES

Directions: First, look at the top set of pictures. These belong together in some way. Next, look at the bottom picture. Then, decide which answer choice would make the bottom set of pictures go together in the same way as the top set. (The small arrow shows that the set goes together.)

Note: Use the same methodology here as Verbal Analogies. Together, come up with a "rule" to describe how the first set is related. (Tip: Try to see what "changes" from the first picture to the second picture.) Then, in the second set, look at the first picture. Take this "rule," use it together with the first picture in the second set, and figure out which of the answer choices follows it. If more than one choice follows this rule, then come up with a rule that is more specific.

You will see similar "rules" with Figure Analogies as with Figure Classification (see p.21). As with Figure Classification, these rules will often involve more than one element. If you have not yet read this section on p.21 , do so now.

Make sure to read through the Answer Key explanations which include additional examples of "rules"/"changes". Also, make sure to go through the checklist at the top of page 9.

Example (#1): In the top left box, the picture shows two shapes. A larger square with vertical, curvy lines and a smaller square with straight, diagonal lines going from upper left to lower right. This smaller square aligns with the left corner of the larger square.

In the top right box, we see the same 2 squares, but what has changed? The smaller square is now aligned with the right corner of the larger square (instead of the left corner). Also, the diagonal lines have changed. They are going from lower left to upper right. The larger square has not changed.

The rule is the smaller shape shifts from left to right and the lines inside switch directions. The larger shape does not change.

The answer where we see this rule is choice B.

1

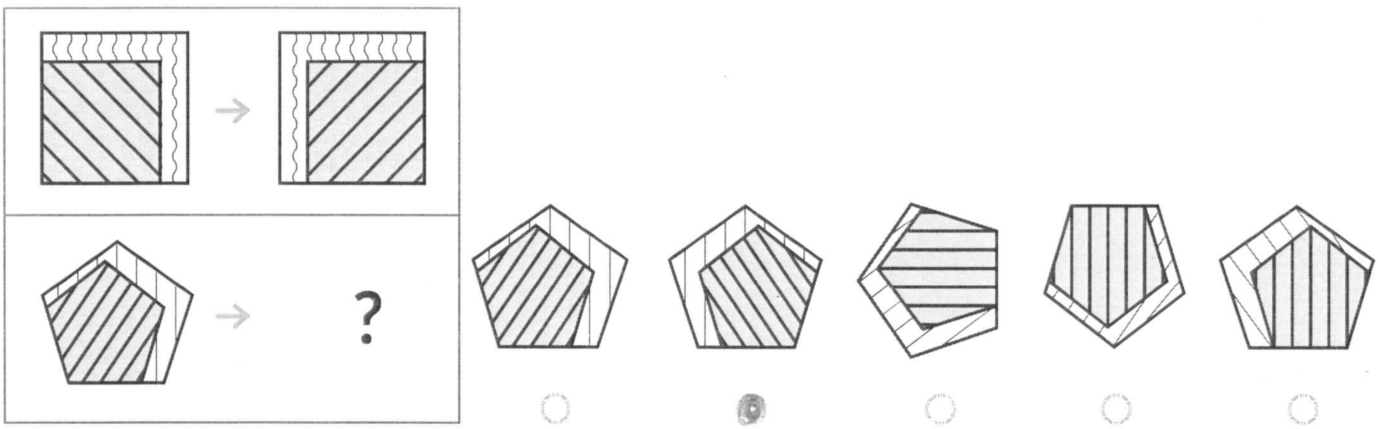

2

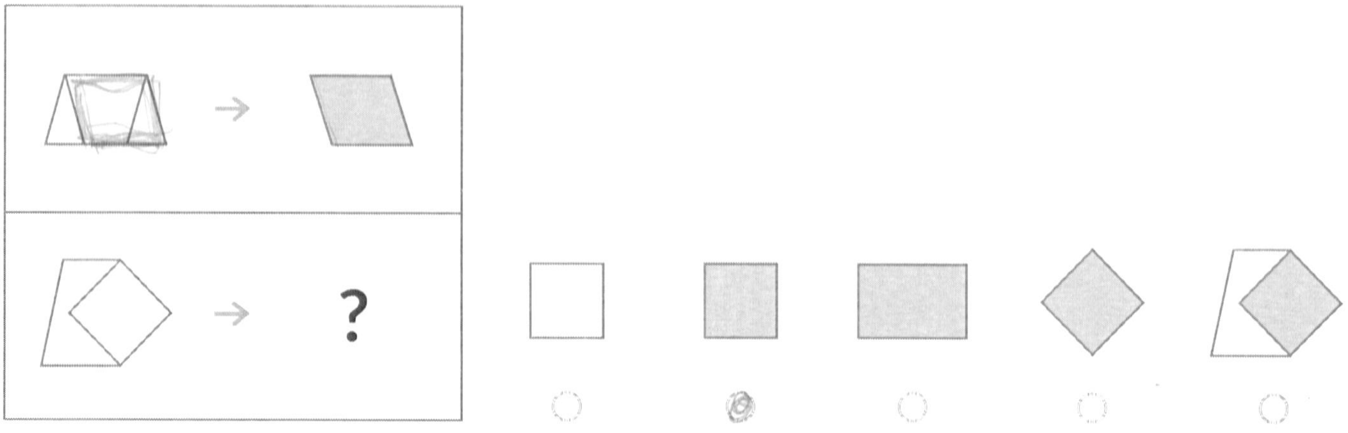

3

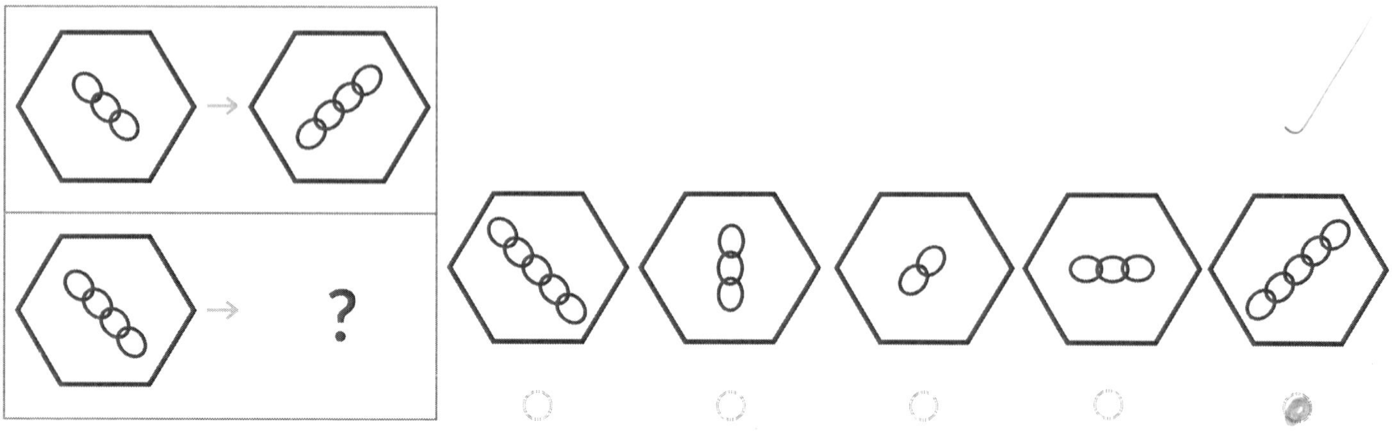

4

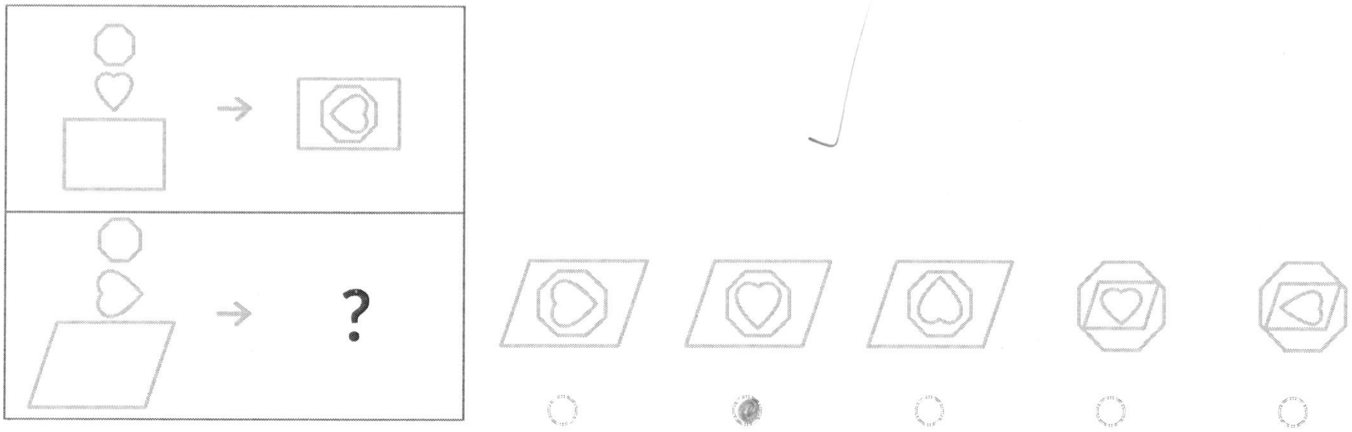

5

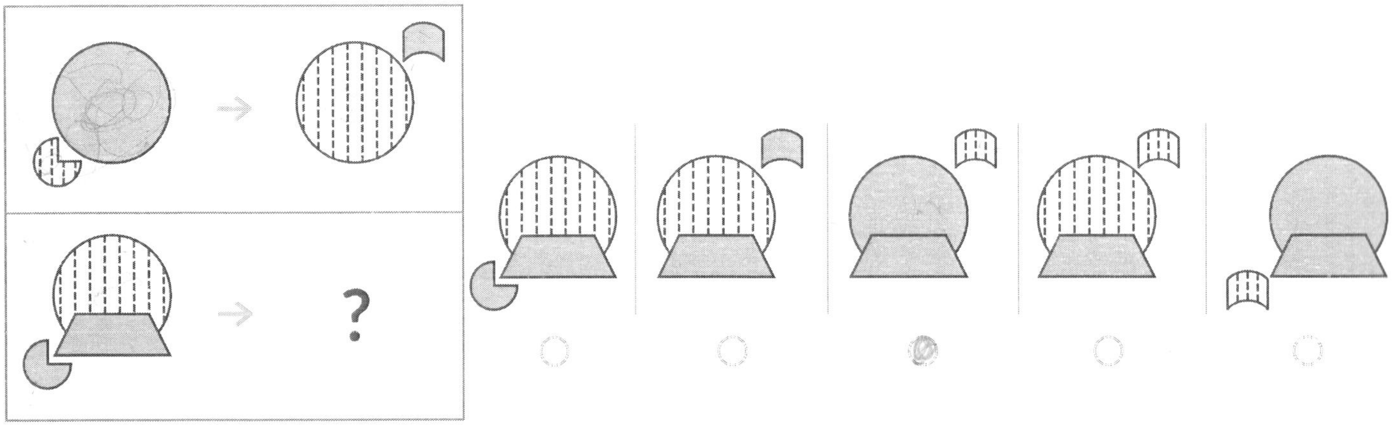

6

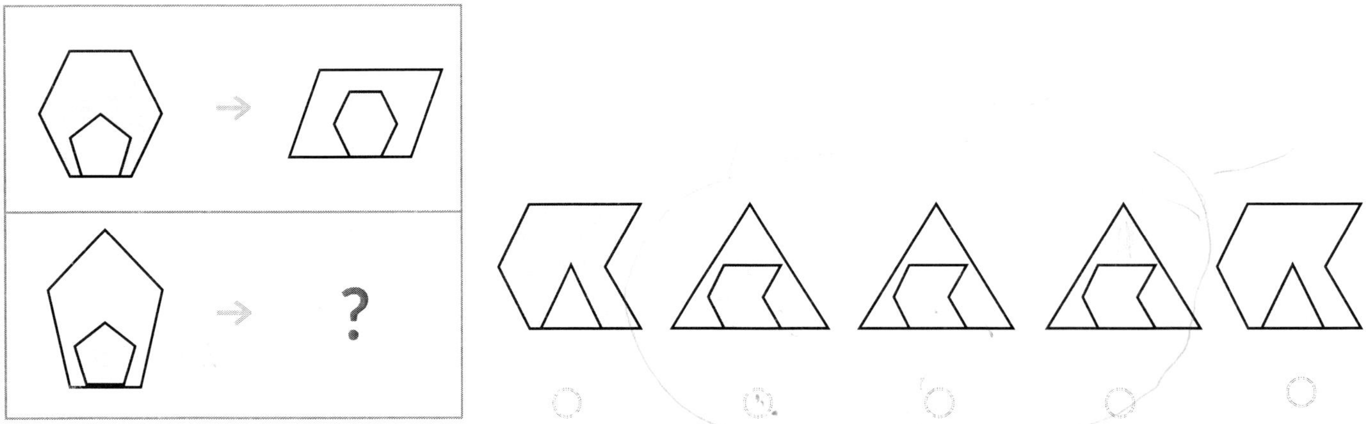

7

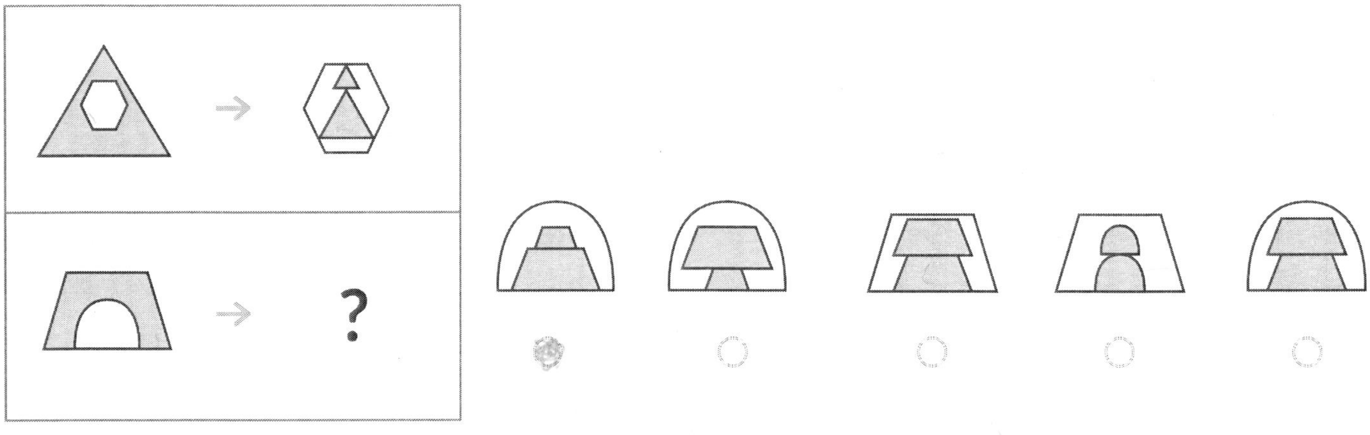

8

9

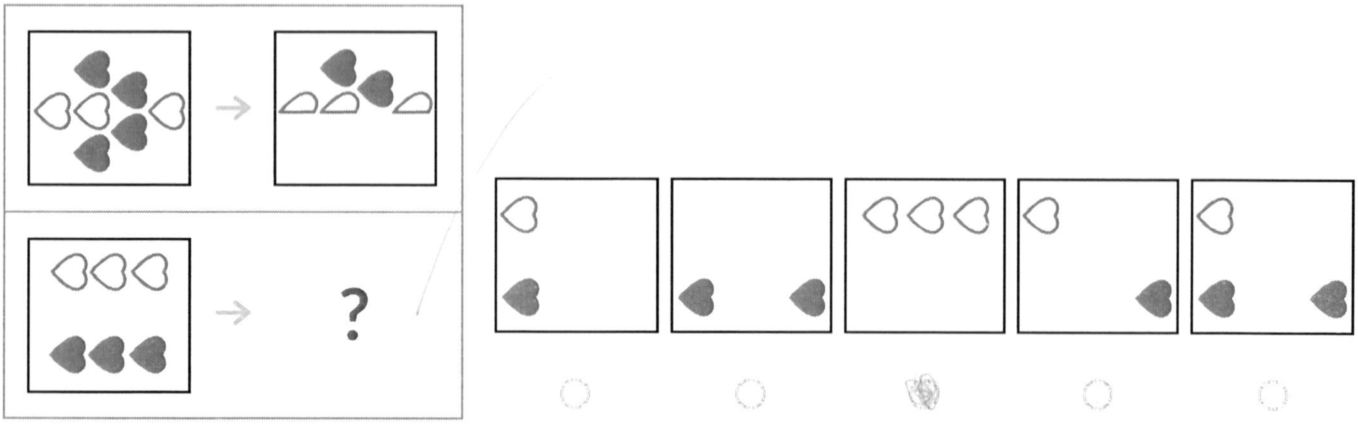

10

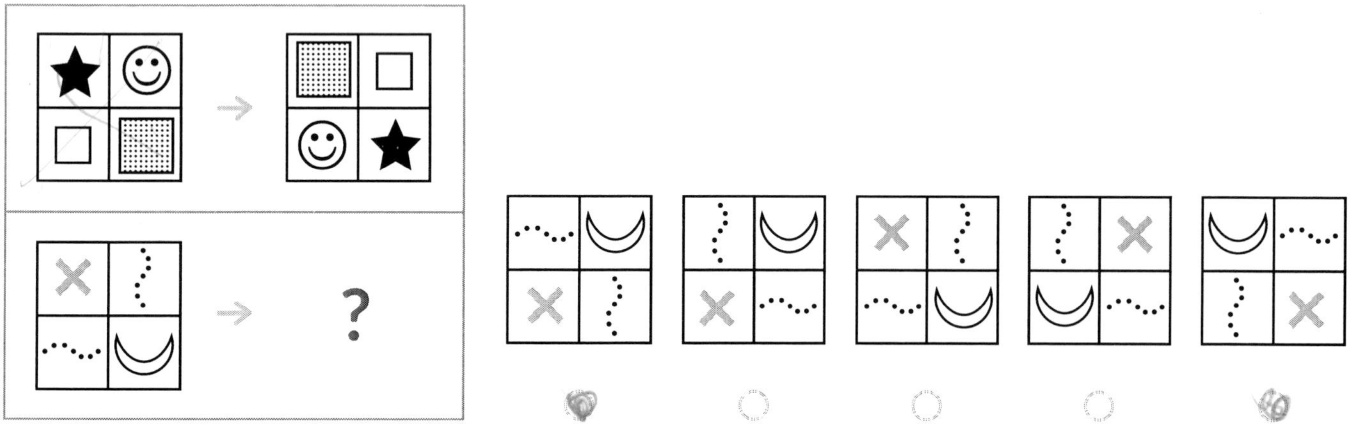

11

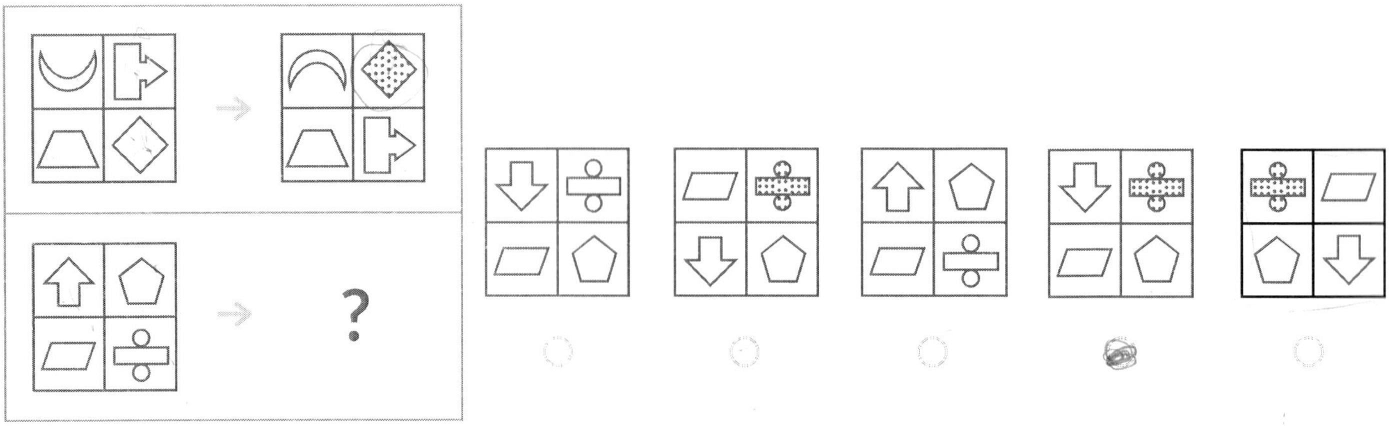

12

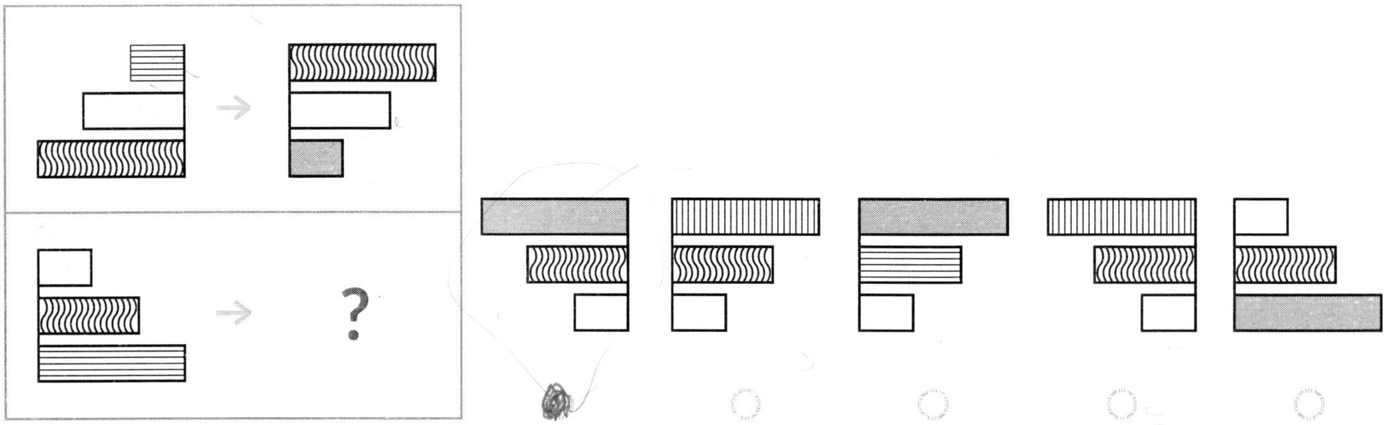

13

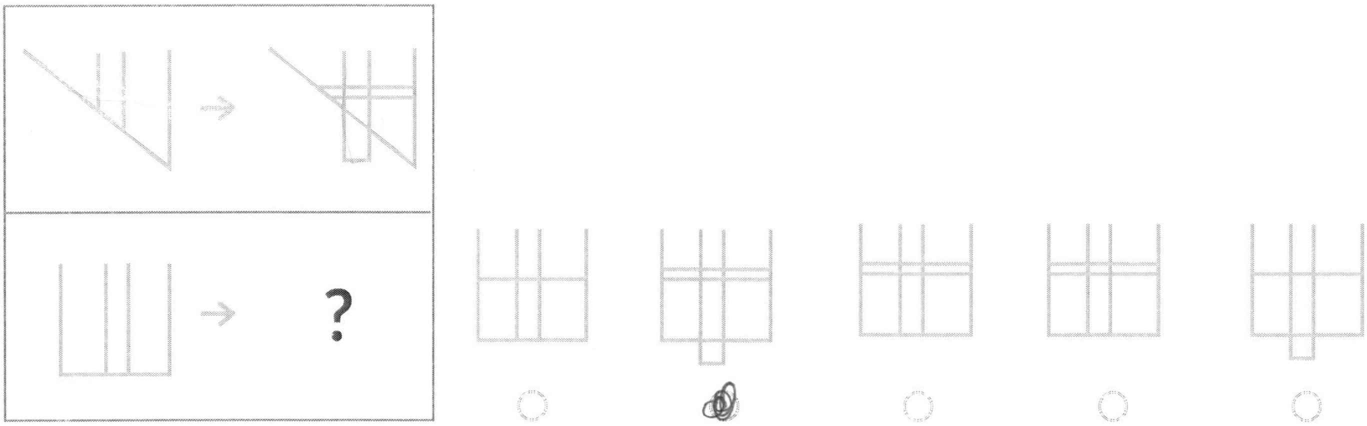

14

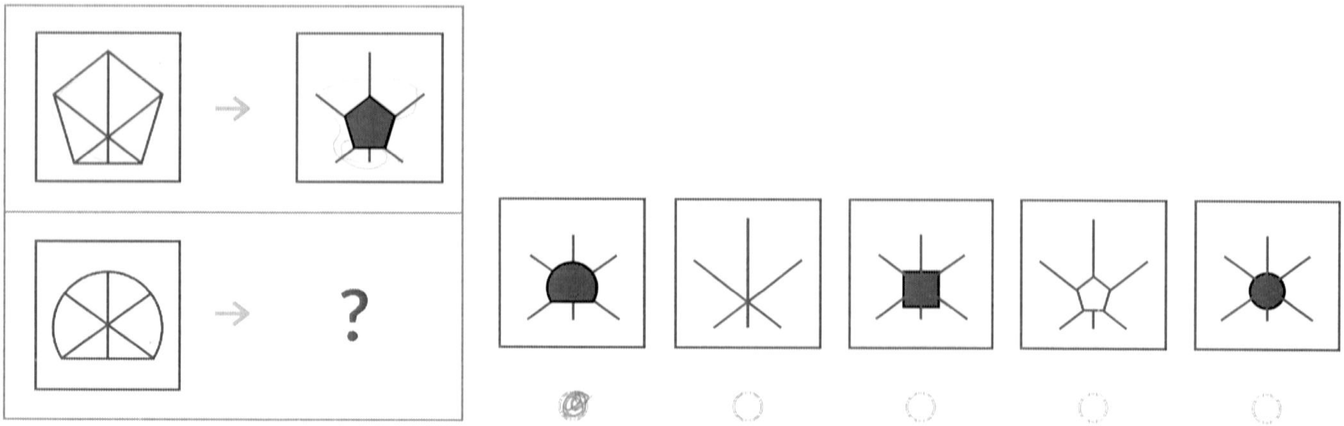

15

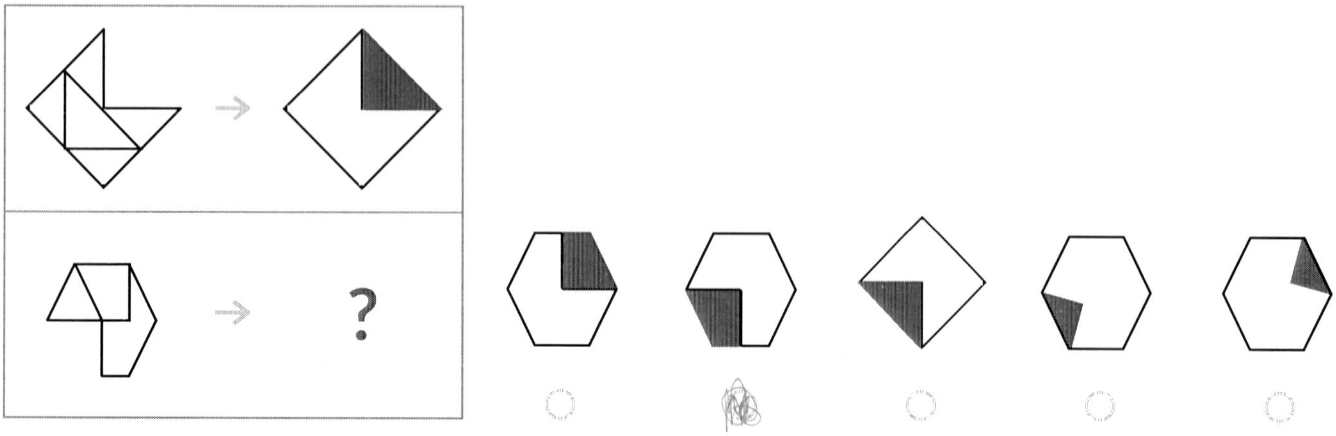

16

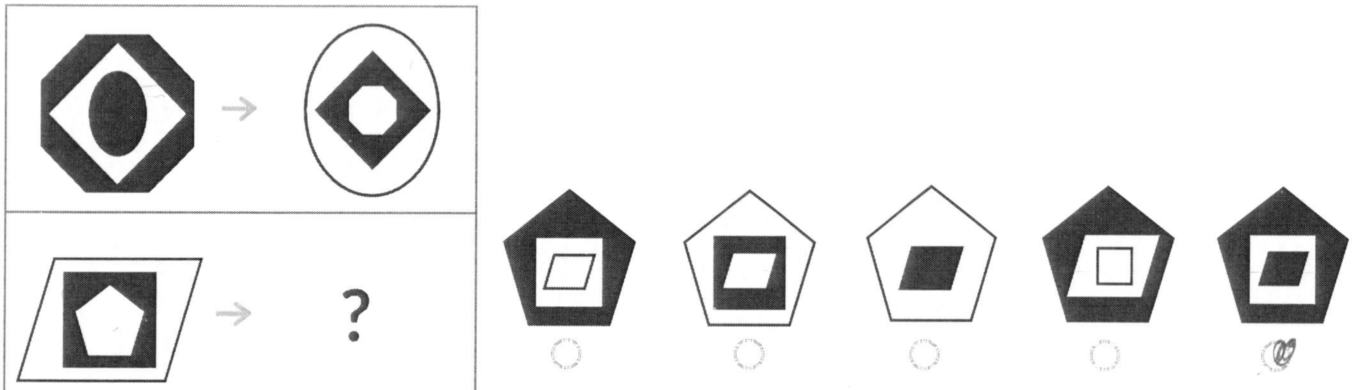

17 with help

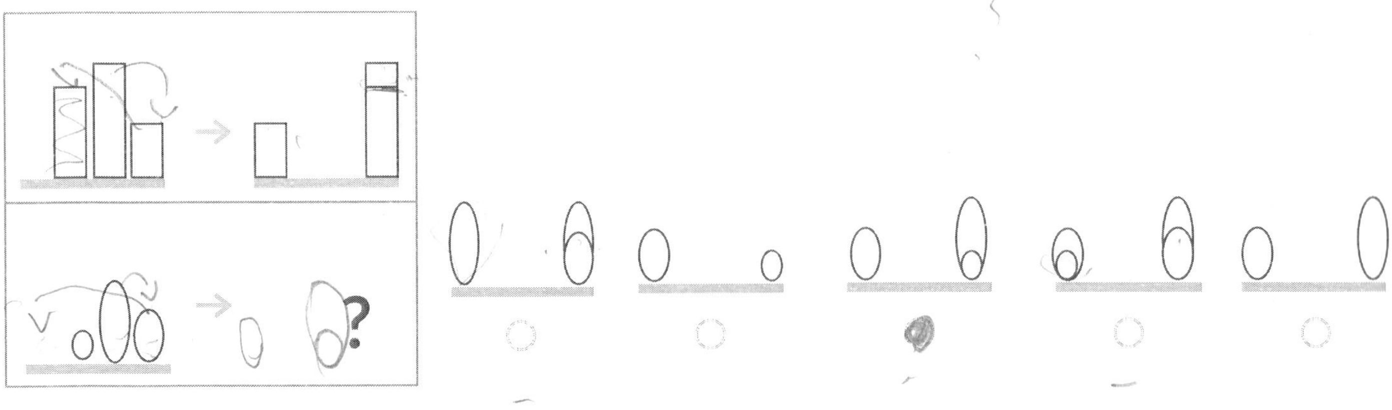

18

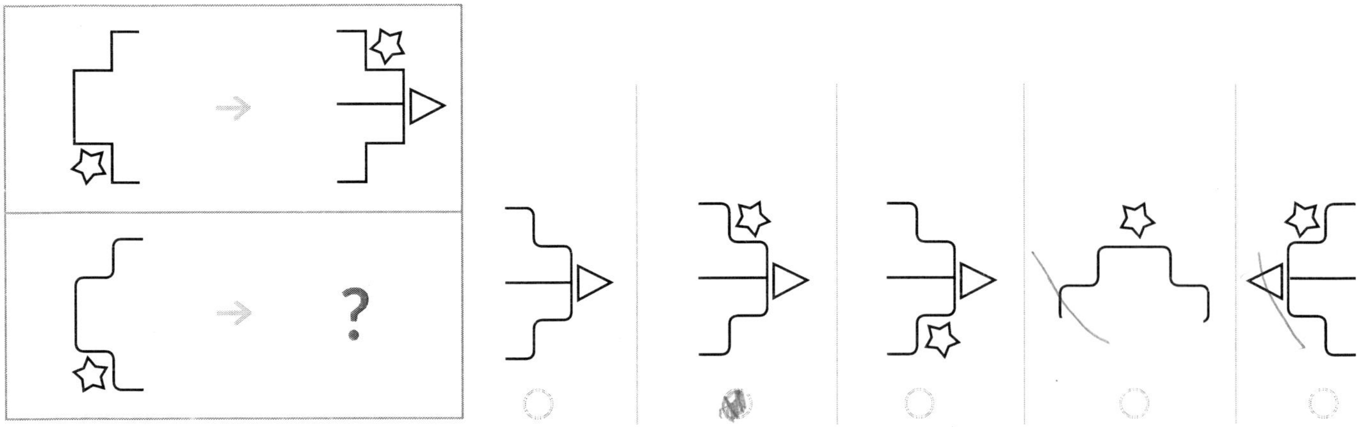

19

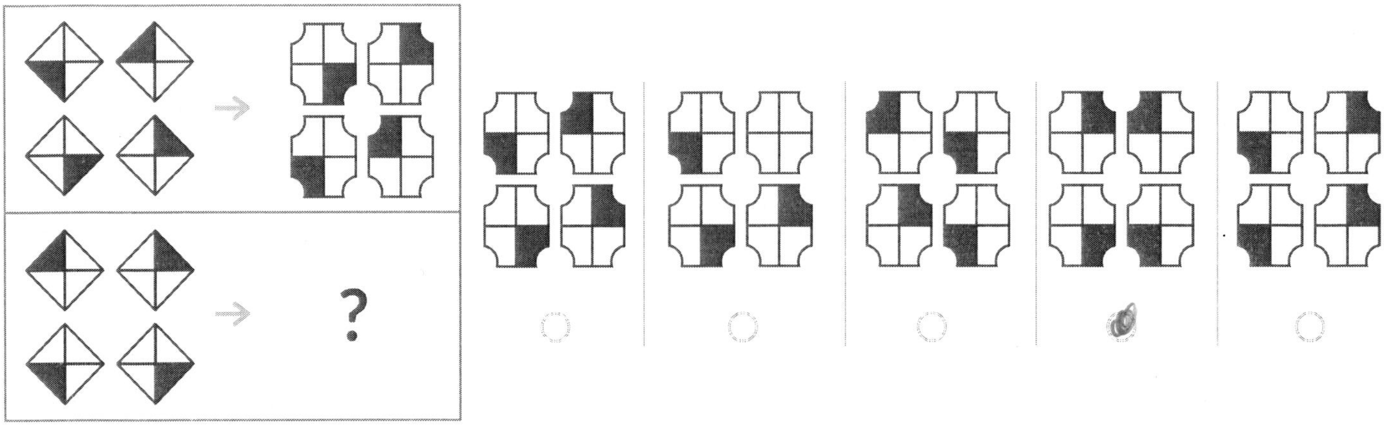

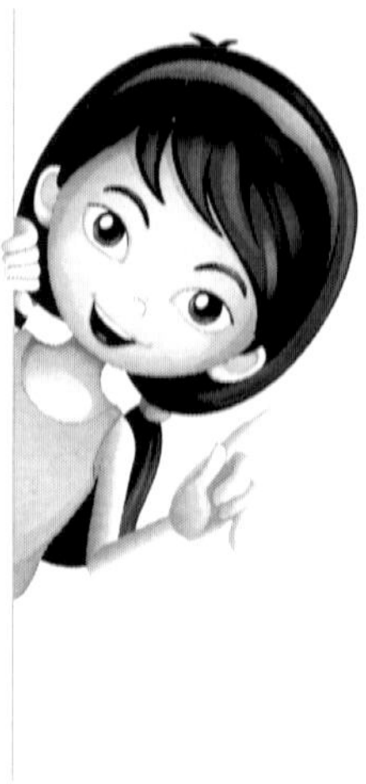

PAPER FOLDING

Directions: The top row of pictures shows a sheet of paper, how it was folded, and then how holes were made in it. Which picture on the bottom row shows how the paper would look after it is unfolded?

Note: To better understand the Paper Folding exercises, you may wish to use real paper and a hole puncher (or scissors). Be sure to notice:

- the number of times the paper is folded (for example, beginning with #6 some questions show paper folded more than once)
- the hole placement
- the number of holes made in the paper

Also, make sure to go through the checklist at the top of page 9.

1

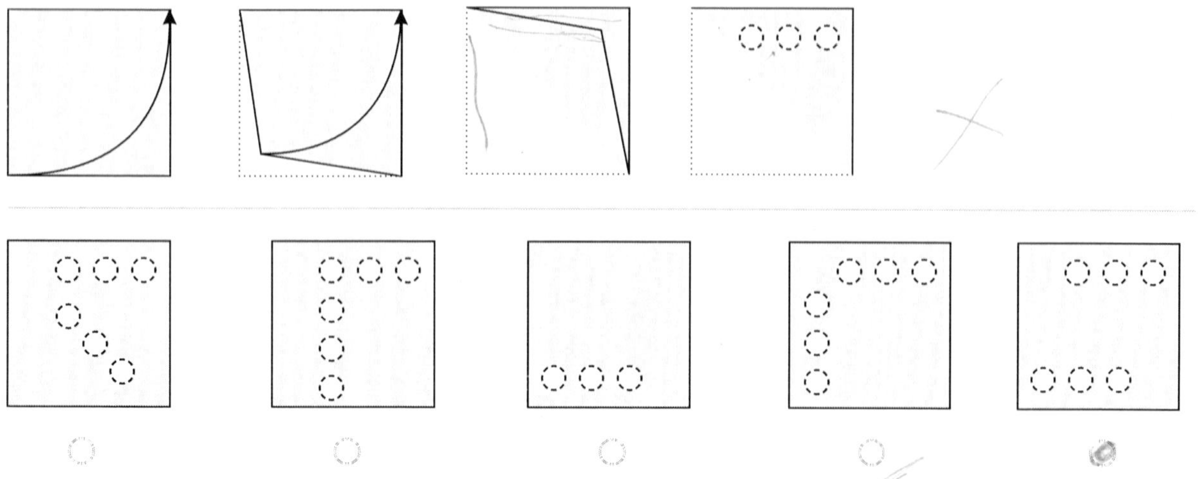

2

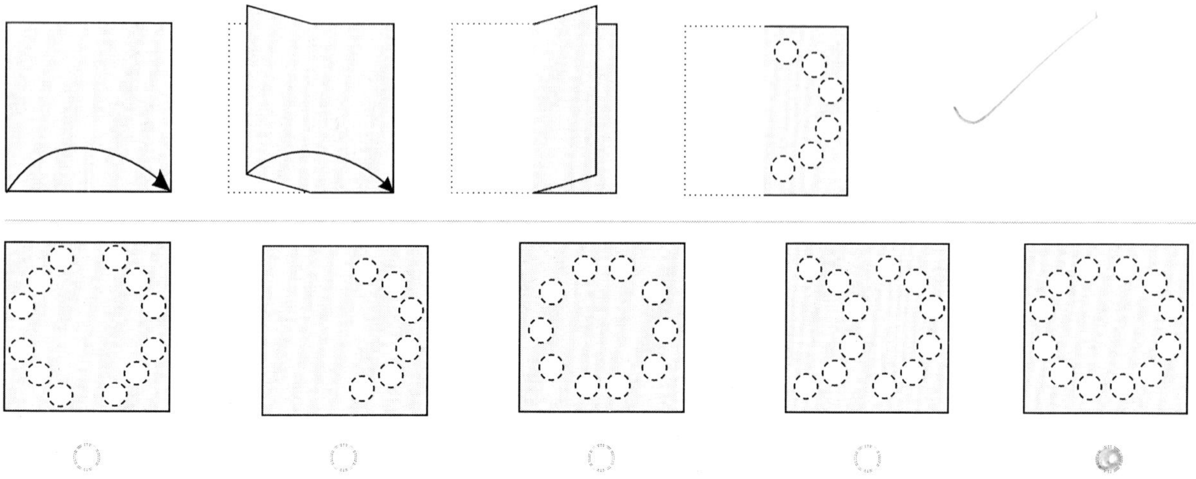

3

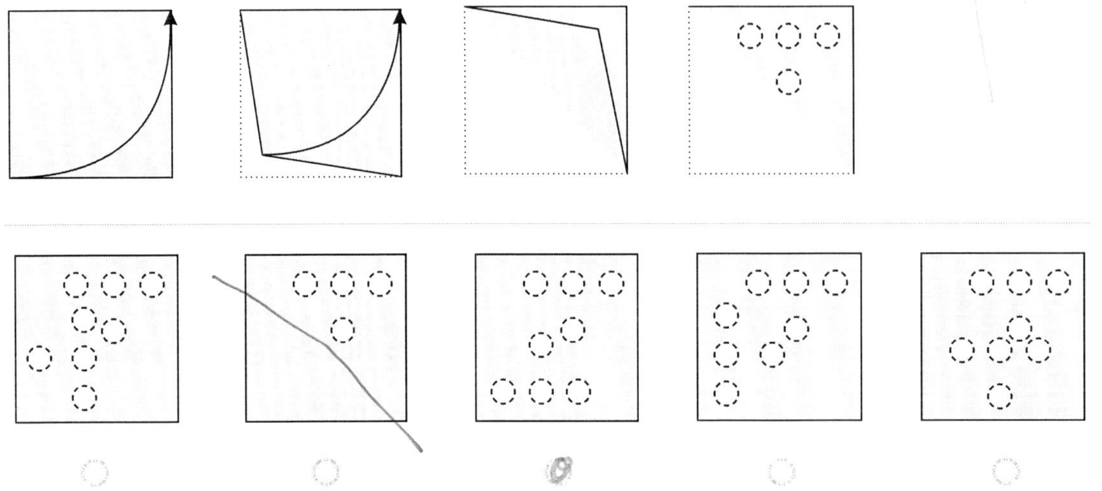

4

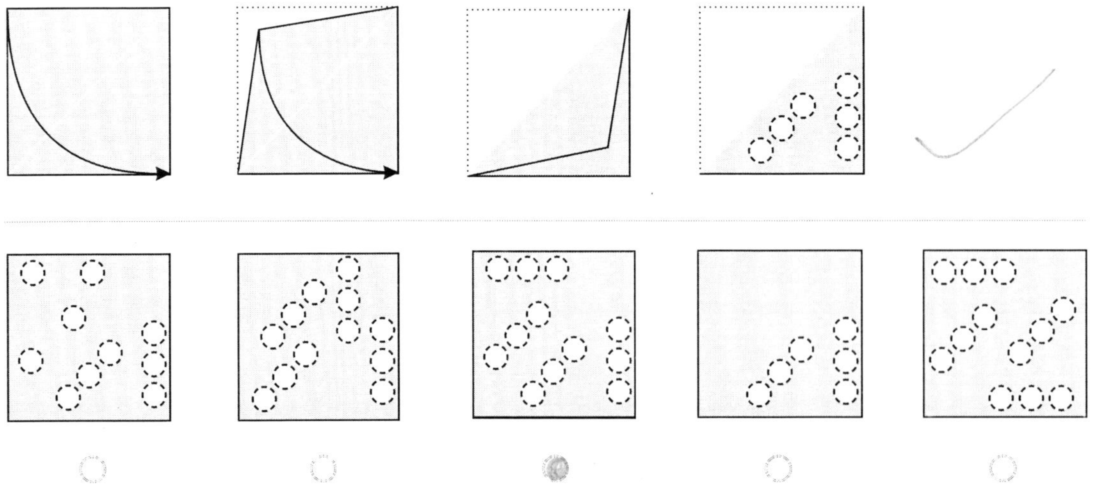

5

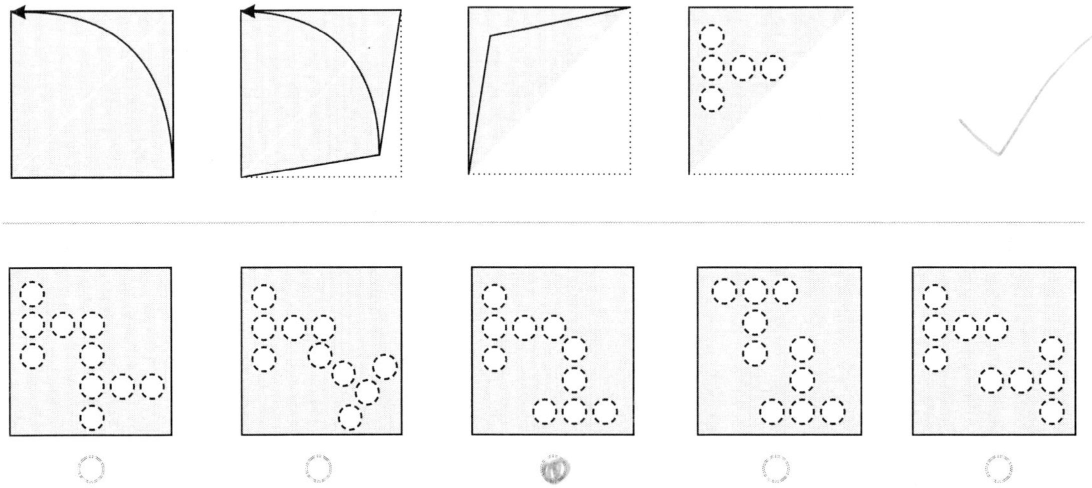

6

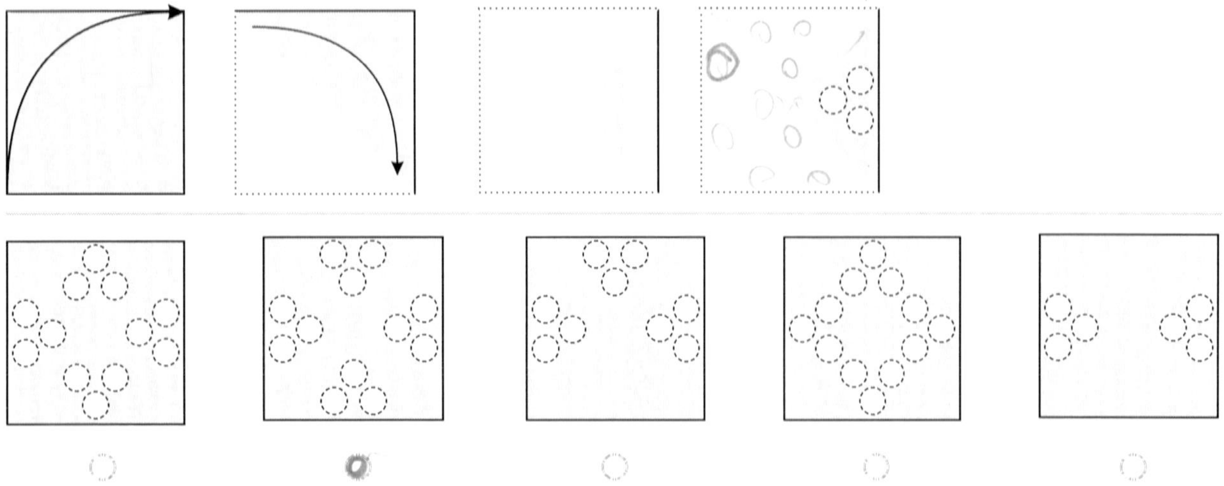

7

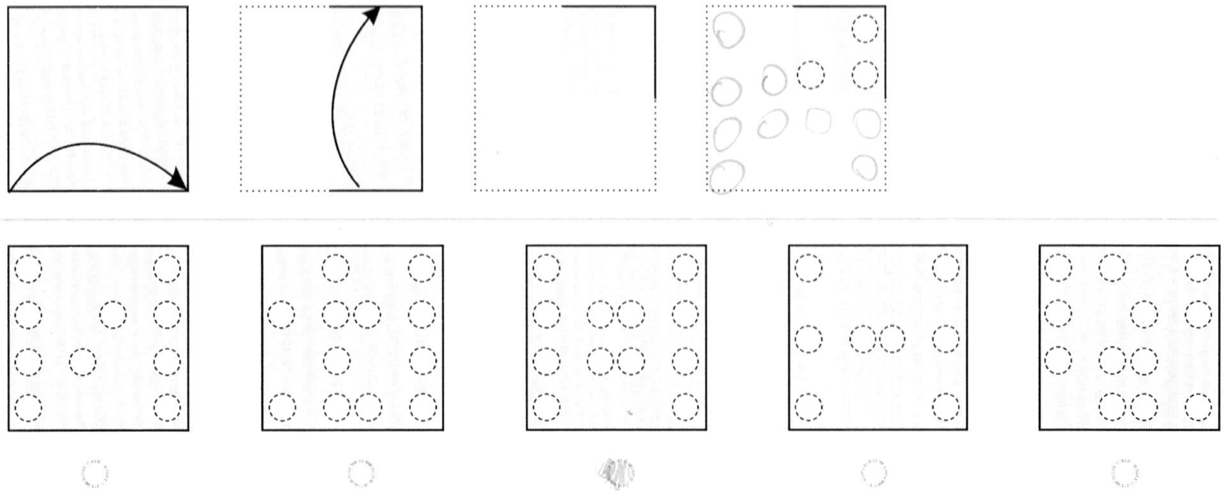

8

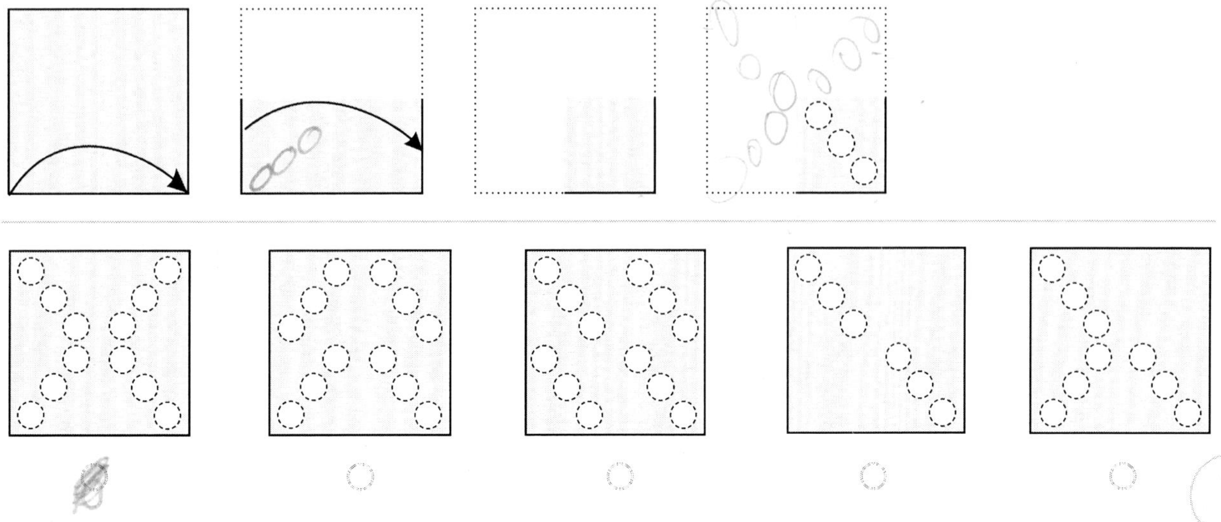

9

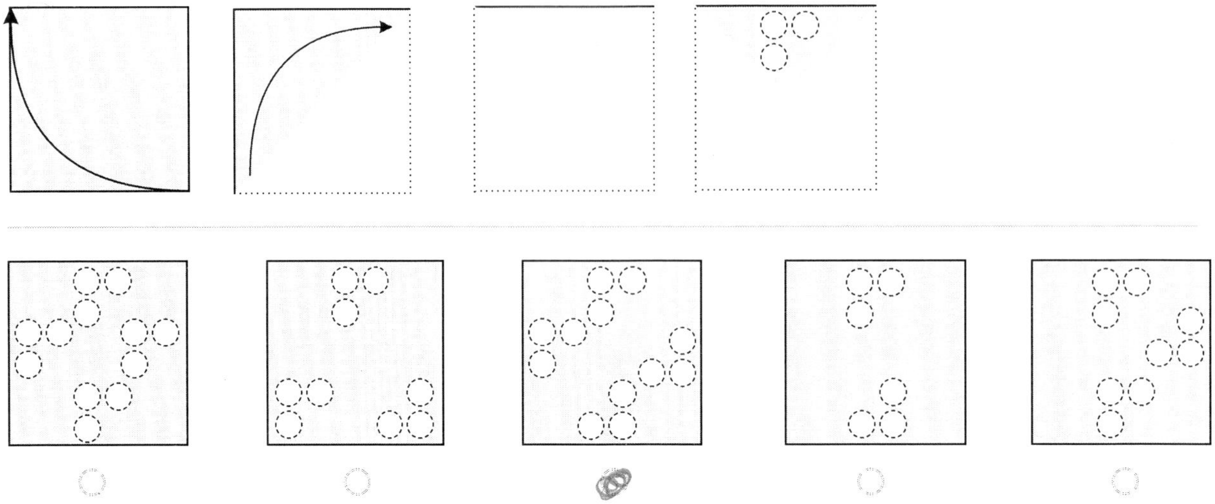

10

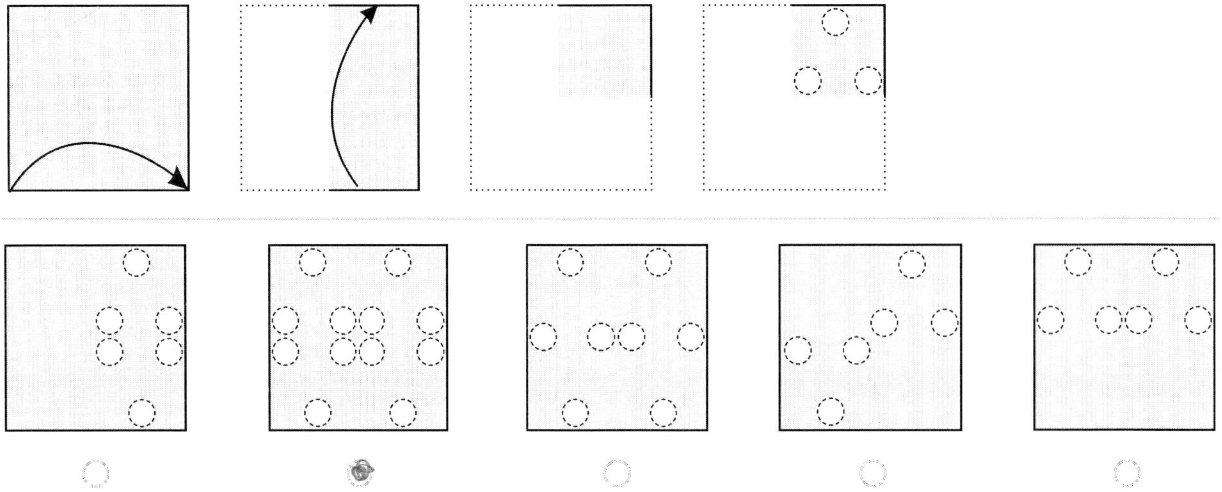

11

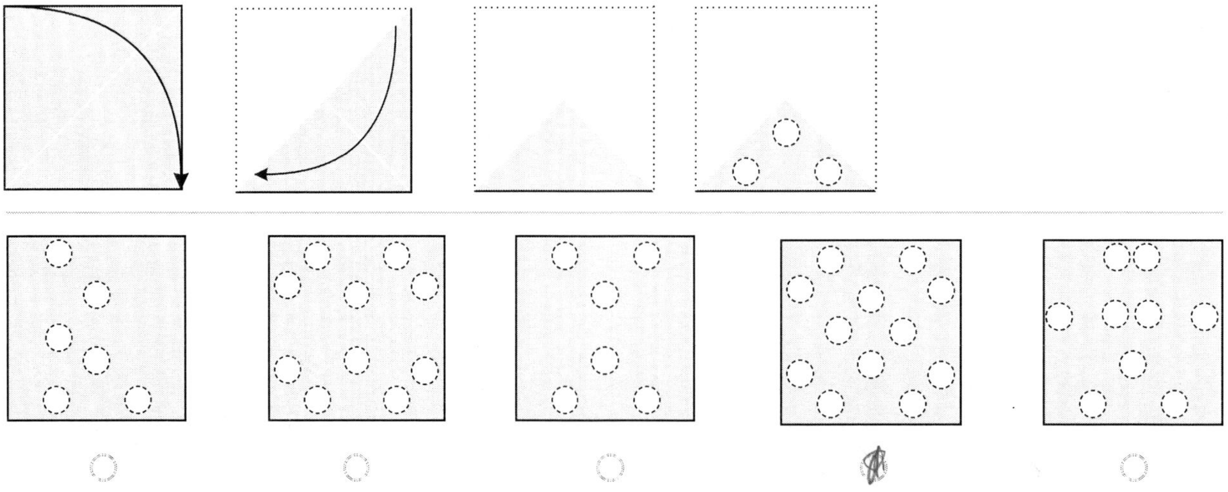

12

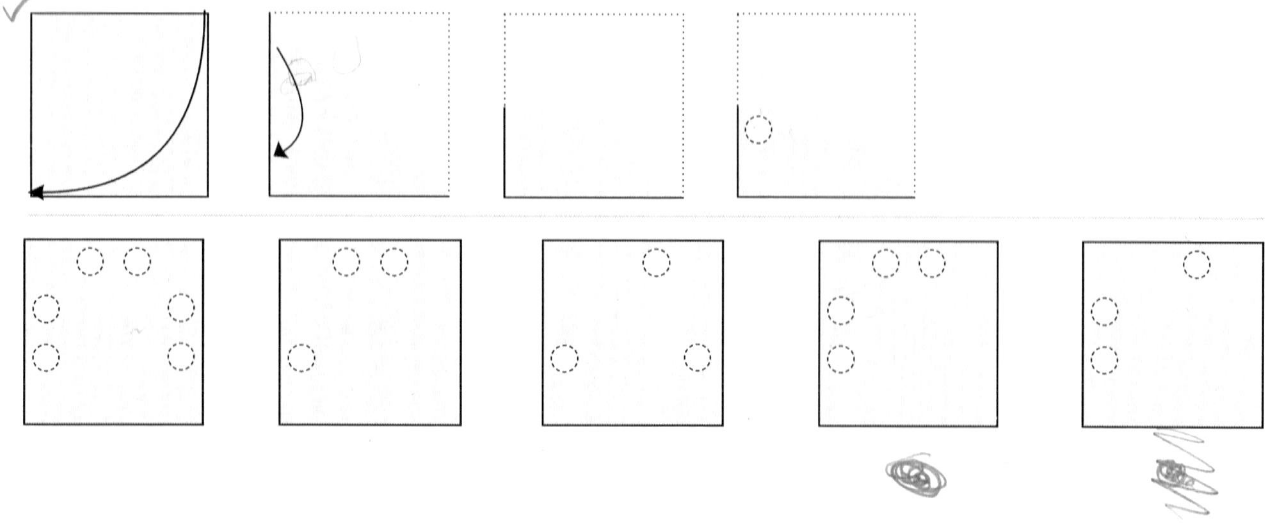

13

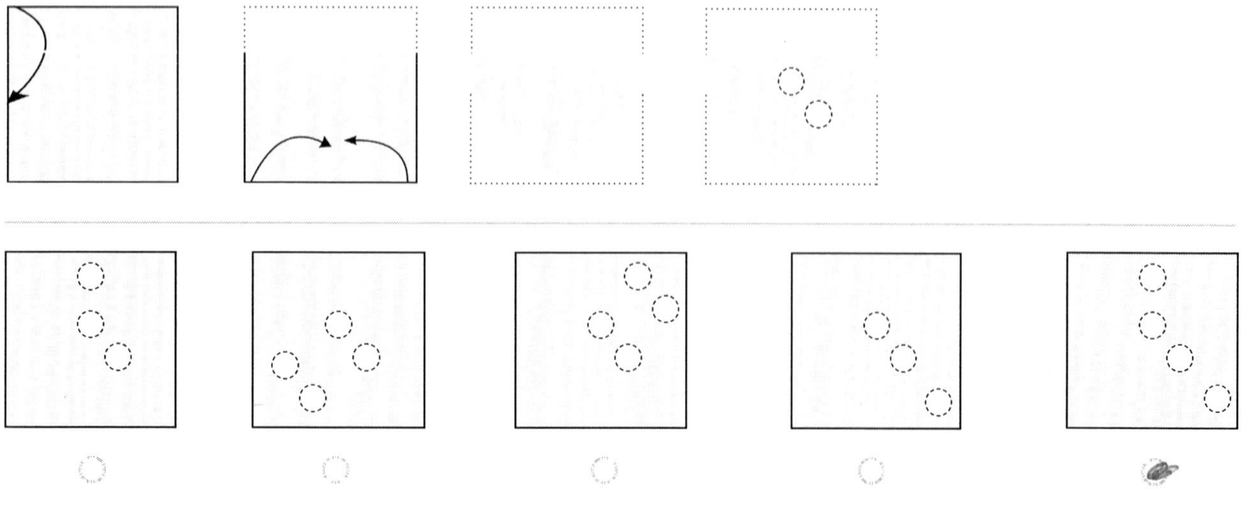

14

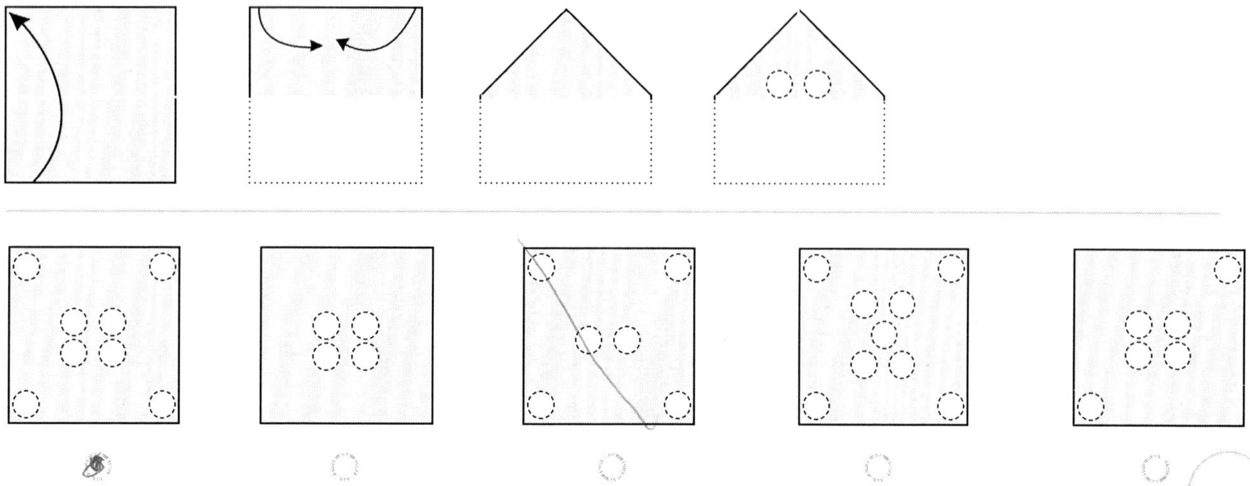

15

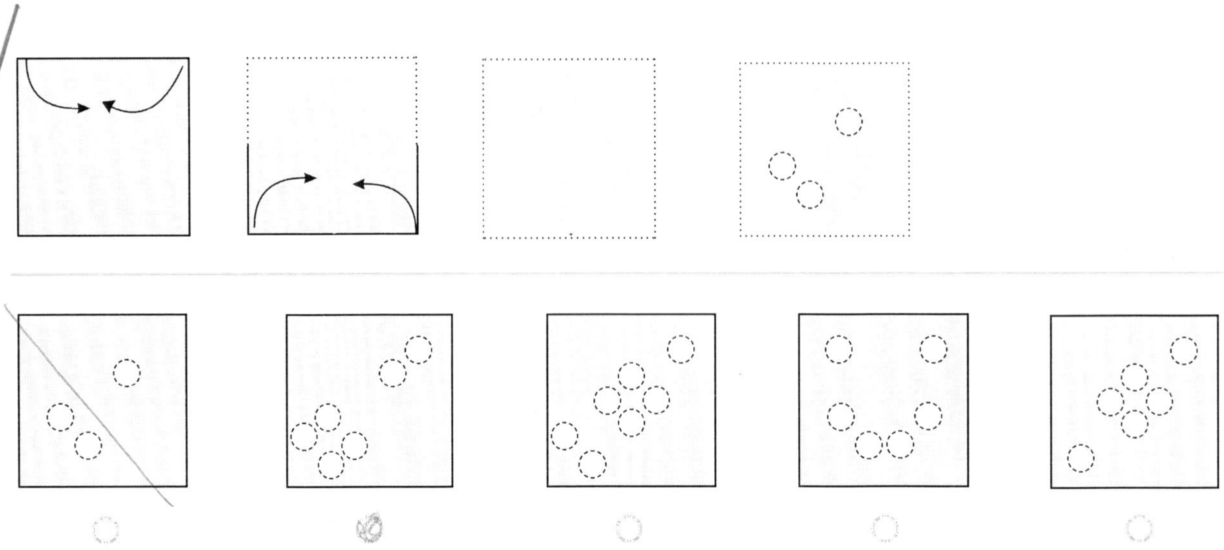

16

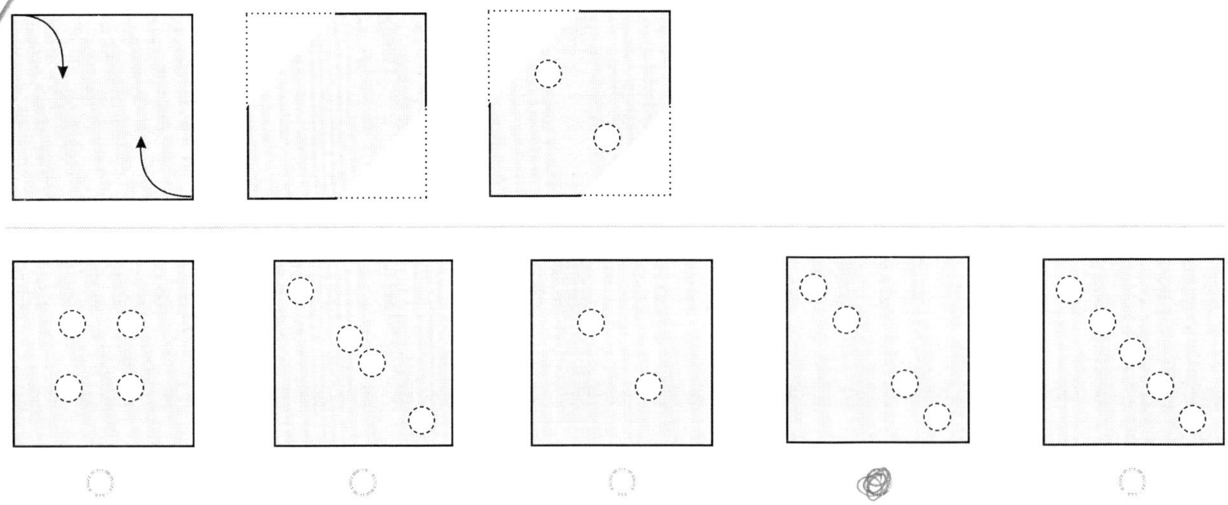

17

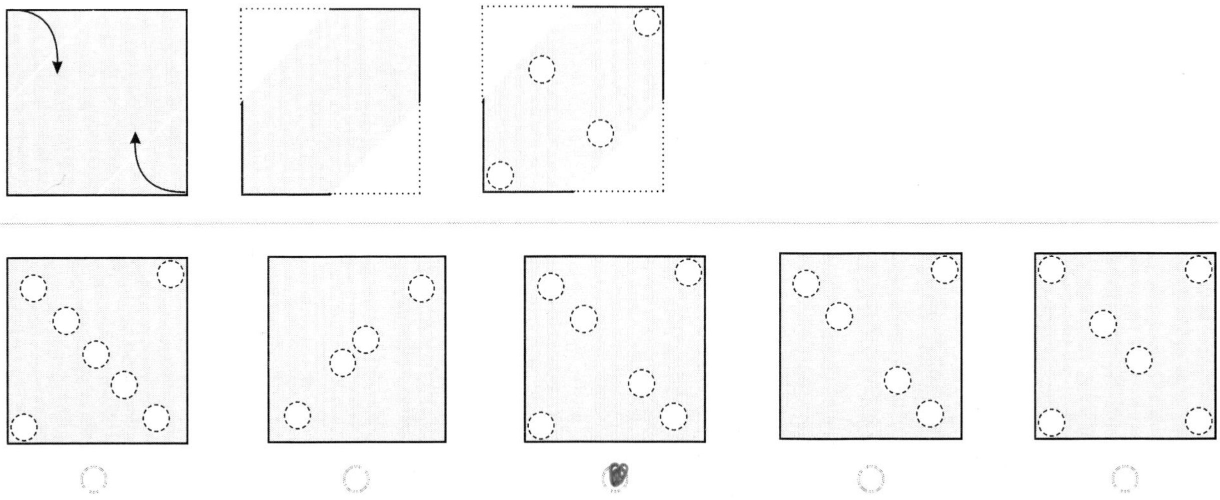

NUMBER PUZZLES

Directions: What answer choice should you put in the place of the question mark so that both sides of the equal sign total the same amount?

Note: As with math problems commonly seen in school, pay close attention to the signs. Do not make the simple mistake of performing the wrong operation (i.e., adding when you should actually be subtracting). Some questions have different operations (i.e., subtracting and division).

Double check your work by replacing the question mark with your answer.

Also, make sure to go through the checklist at the top of page 9.

Example 1: The left side of the equal sign totals 32. Which answer choice do you need to put in the place of the question mark so that the right side of the equal sign totals 32? 4 times what number equals 32? 4 times 8 equals 32. So, the answer is 8.

Example 2: First, we need to replace the diamond with the correct number. We need to replace the diamond with 19. We see that the right side of the equation equals 21. What number do we need to put in place of the question mark so that the left side also equals 21? 40 minus 19 equals 21. So, the answer is 40.

1   **32 = 4 x [?]**

○ 36   ○ 10   ○ 8   ○ 28   ○ 9

2   **[?] - ◆ = 21**

◆ = 19

○ 50   ○ 2   ○ 30   ○ 20   ○ 40

3

$$54 = 9 \times \boxed{?}$$

- 9
- 63
- 45
- 6
- 7

4

$$32 = 128 \div \boxed{?}$$

- 32
- 4
- 96
- 14
- 160

5

$$\boxed{?} = 52 \div 2$$

- 26
- 50
- 21
- 48
- 54

6

$$42 \div 7 = 21 - \boxed{?}$$

- 29
- 15
- 28
- 17
- 6

7

$$5 \times 8 = 11 + \boxed{?}$$

- 19
- 29
- 2
- 12
- 40

8

$$40 \div 8 = \boxed{?} \div 3$$

○ 16 ○ 45 ○ 7 ○ 15 ○ 5

9

$$12 \times 3 = \boxed{?} \times 4$$

○ 9 ○ 13 ○ 5 ○ 8 ○ 36

10

$$3 + \boxed{?} = \blacklozenge$$

$$2 + \blacklozenge = 10$$

○ 11 ○ 2 ○ 8 ○ 15 ○ 5

11

$$5 + \boxed{?} = \blacklozenge$$

$$6 + \blacklozenge = 13$$

○ 35 ○ 2 ○ 10 ○ 3 ○ 7

12

$$\boxed{?} + 1 = 2 \times \blacklozenge$$

$$3 = \blacklozenge - 4$$

○ 14 ○ 6 ○ 15 ○ 13 ○ 7

13

$\boxed{?} + 2 = 3 \times \blacklozenge$

$2 = \blacklozenge - 1$

○ 2 ○ 3 ○ 7 ○ 9 ○ 27

14

$4 + \boxed{?} = 2 \times \blacklozenge$

$\blacklozenge - 1 = 6$

○ 16 ○ 7 ○ 2 ○ 10 ○ 14

15

$4 + \boxed{?} = 5 \times \blacklozenge$

$\blacklozenge + 6 = 9$

○ 11 ○ 21 ○ 1 ○ 15 ○ 9

16

$\boxed{?} = \blacklozenge - 2$

$\bullet = \blacklozenge + 1$

$\bullet = 4$

○ 5 ○ 1 ○ 2 ○ 3 ○ 0

17

$\boxed{?} = \blacklozenge - 4$

$\bullet = \blacklozenge \times 2$

$\bullet = 12$

○ 18 ○ 6 ○ 10 ○ 24 ○ 2

NUMBER ANALOGIES

Directions Look at the first two sets of numbers. Come up with a rule that both of these sets follow. Take this rule to figure out which answer choice goes in the place of the question mark.

Parent note: As with Verbal Analogies, your child must try to come up with a "rule" to answer the question. It must work with *all* the pairs. Be sure to test it on each one. The "rule" will involve standard math operations (subtraction, addition, division, or multiplication).

Also, the more challenging questions will involve *two operations*. These types of questions start at #13. For example, #13 involves multiplication *and* addition. To arrive at the second number in the pair, you must multiply the first number by 2. Once you have done this, then you must add 1.

With all of the Number Analogies questions (as with all questions), it is very important to double check your work to ensure each number pair (and then the answer) follows the rule.

Also, make sure to go through the checklist at the top of page 9.

Example #1: In the first two sets you have 30 and 22, 47 and 39. How would you get from 30 to 22? How would you get from 47 to 39? In each, you subtract 8 from the first number. This is the "rule". Take this rule, look at the number at the beginning of the third set (25) and apply it to the bottom row of answer choices. What is the answer when you subtract 8 from 25? The answer is 17.

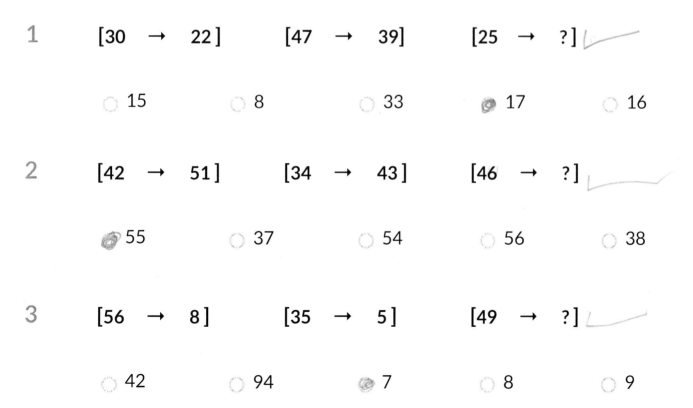

1 [30 → 22] [47 → 39] [25 → ?]

○ 15 ○ 8 ○ 33 ○ 17 ○ 16

2 [42 → 51] [34 → 43] [46 → ?]

○ 55 ○ 37 ○ 54 ○ 56 ○ 38

3 [56 → 8] [35 → 5] [49 → ?]

○ 42 ○ 94 ○ 7 ○ 8 ○ 9

4 [6 → 48] [9 → 72] [8 → ?]

- 16
- 56
- 80
- 24
- 64

5 [7 → 3 1/2] [9 → 4 1/2] [11 → ?]

- 11 1/2
- 6
- 5 1/2
- 10
- 1/2

6 [3 → 9] [2 → 4] [5 → ?]

- 5
- 25
- 15
- 51
- 10

7 [1/4 → 1/2] [3/4 → 1] [1/2 → ?]

- 1/3
- 2/4
- 3/4
- 0
- 1/8

8 [0.3 → 0.03] [0.5 → 0.05] [1 → ?]

- 0.1
- 0.01
- 1
- 10
- 10.1

9 √ [2/8 → 1/4] [3/6 → 1/2] [3/9 → ?]

- 1/9
- 1/3
- 1/2
- 1/4
- 1/5

10 √ [70 → 7] [40 → 4] [100 → ?]

- 110
- 1
- 5
- 10
- 15

11 √ [65 → 52] [26 → 13] [41 → ?]

-13 -13

- 13
- 14
- 54
- 26
- 28

12 √ [48 → 80] [39 → 71] [38 → ?]

+32 +32

- 32
- 74
- 70
- 72
- 6

13 X [2 → 5] [3 → 7] [5 → ?]

- 7
- 11
- 10
- 9
- 16

14 [5 → 26] [6 → 31] [8 → ?]

○ 33 ○ 40 ○ 39 ○ 13 ○ 41

15 [2 → 8] [4 → 14] [7 → ?]

○ 21 ○ 2 ○ 12 ○ 23 ○ 19

16 [8 → 33] [6 → 25] [9 → ?]

○ 14 ○ 4 ○ 37 ○ 28 ○ 36

17 [13 → 28] [0 → 2] [16 → ?]

○ 31 ○ 36 ○ 34 ○ 20 ○ 18

18 [9 → 46] [8 → 41] [6 → ?]

○ 12 ○ 31 ○ 0 ○ 39 ○ 25

19 [9 → 37] [11 → 45] [10 → ?]

○ 31 ○ 44 ○ 39 ○ 15 ○ 41

20 [6 → 4] [4 → 3] [8 → ?]

○ 6 ○ 7 ○ 4 ○ 5 ○ 11

21 [3 → 2] [12 → 5] [9 → ?]

○ 4 ○ 5 ○ 2 ○ 13 ○ 6

22 [22 → 12] [40 → 21] [36 → ?]

○ 26 ○ 17 ○ 19 ○ 18 ○ 33

23 [21 → 8] [30 → 11] [39 → ?]

○ 26 ○ 14 ○ 20 ○ 43 ○ 35

NUMBER SERIES

Directions: Here, you must try to figure out a pattern that the numbers have made. Which answer choice would complete the pattern?

Note: As with other questions types, it is helpful to figure out a "rule" that the numbers have made. In this section, it is a pattern. Use the "rule" / pattern to figure out the missing number. As with the Number Analogies, the rules will involve subtraction, addition, division, or multiplication.

Some of these are quite challenging and involve more than one "rule". They could even involve more than one kind of operation (addition/ subtraction/ multiplication/ division). For example, the pattern in #4 involves two different numbers (+1, +7). The pattern in #9 involves different numbers and operations (+2, -3).

Double check your work to ensure the series of numbers (and then the answer) follows the rule / pattern.

Also, make sure to go through the checklist at the top of page 9.

Example #1: Do you see a pattern or a rule that the numbers in the series follow? How do you get from 51 to 43, then from 43 to 35, then from 35 to 27, then from 27 to 19, and finally from 19 to 11? Each time, each number decreases by 8. If this is the pattern, then what would come after 11? It's Choice D, 3.

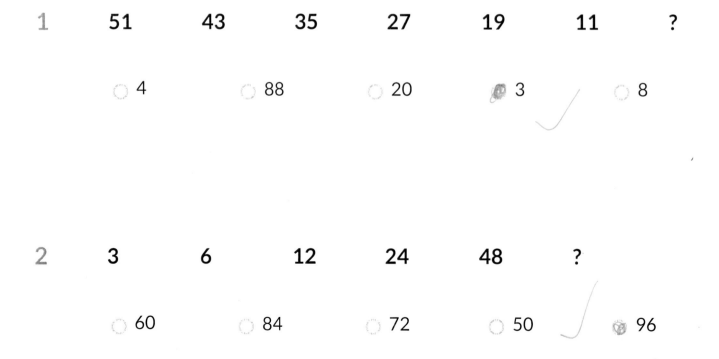

1 **51 43 35 27 19 11 ?**

○ 4 ○ 88 ○ 20 ○ 3 ○ 8

2 **3 6 12 24 48 ?**

○ 60 ○ 84 ○ 72 ○ 50 ○ 96

3 **2 18 34 50 66 ?**

○ 92 ○ 60 ○ 72 ● 82 ○ 80

4 **3 4 11 12 19 20 27 ?**

○ 30 ● 28 ○ 10 ○ 26 ○ 34

5 **2 4 7 11 16 22 29 ?**

● 37 ○ 34 ○ 10 ○ 11 ○ 35

6 **30 28 25 23 20 18 15 ?**

○ 28 ○ 10 ● 13 ○ 17 ○ 12

7 **5 11 5 12 5 13 ?**

● 5 ○ 14 ○ 18 ○ 8 ○ 26

8 51 43 36 30 25 21 18 ?

○ 11 ○ 16 ○ 10 ○ 17 ○ 22

9 10 12 9 11 8 10 7 ?

○ 9 ○ 6 ○ 11 ○ 4 ○ 19

10 5 8 14 21 24 30 37 40 46 ?

○ 50 ○ 53 ○ 49 ○ 64 ○ 60

11 144 72 36 18 ?

○ 20 ○ 0 ○ 12 ○ 9 ○ 16

12 1 4 2 8 4 16 8 32 ?

○ 28 ○ 30 ○ 64 ○ 4 ○ 16

13 3 5 7 6 8 10 9 11 13 ?

- 10
- 3
- 12
- 14
- 16

14 72.01 72.06 72.11 72.16 72.21 72.26 ?

- 72.31
- 72.62
- 72.72
- 77.26
- 77.06

15 75 70 64 57 52 46 39 34 28 ?

- 20
- 35
- 22
- 20
- 21

16 7 18 7 22 7 26 7 ?

- 28
- 14
- 22
- 30
- 7

17 20 25 17 19 24 16 18 23 15 ?

- 24
- 25
- 27
- 13
- 17

18 4 10 1 5 11 2 6 12 3 ?

○ 4 ○ 7 ○ 10 ○ 13 ○ 9

19 35 25 33 31 21 29 27 17 25 ?

○ 33 ○ 20 ○ 23 ○ 13 ○ 15

20 21 14 23 19 12 21 17 10 19 ?

○ 20 ○ 18 ○ 12 ○ 23 ○ 15

21 64 39 72 39 80 39 ?

○ 88 ○ 60 ○ 76 ○ 80 ○ 39

22 2 3 4 3 6 9 6 10 14 ?

○ 9 ○ 18 ○ 13 ○ 10 ○ 2

23 3 6 12 6 12 24 12 24 48 ?

○ 24 ○ 8.0 ○ 10.0 ○ 9.5 ○ 10.5

End of Practice Test 1 (Workbook Format). • Practice Test 2 begins on the next page.

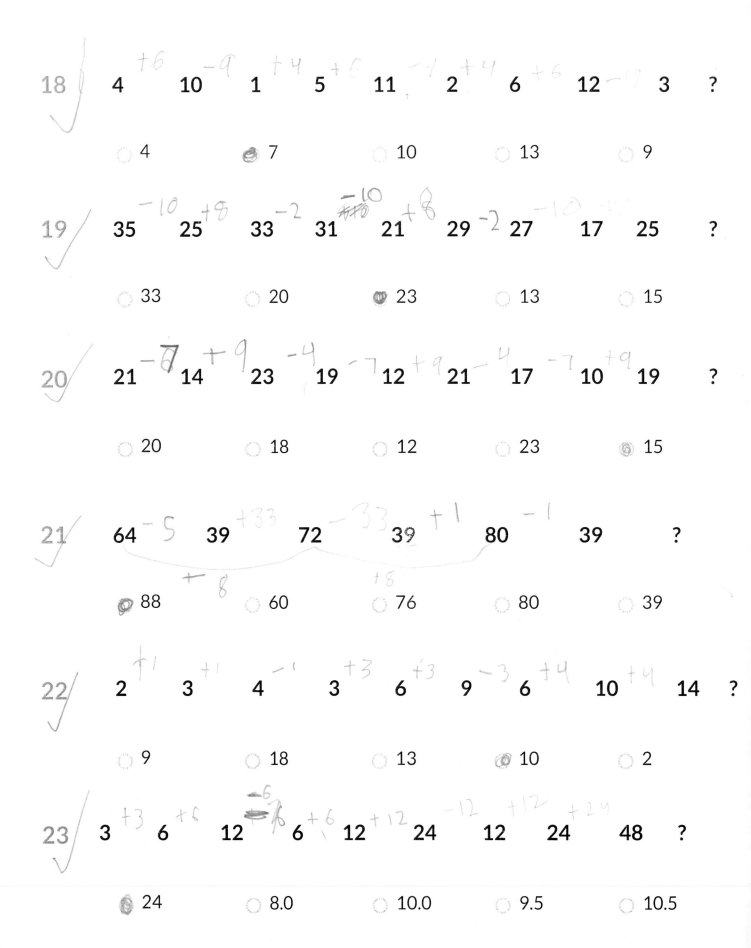

131/167

Directions: Which choice makes the second set of words go together in the same way as the first set?

12/20

1 **cells → body : words →**

(A) vowel (B) alphabet (C) syllable (D) book (E) consonant

2 **blood → artery : water →**

(A) wet (B) rain (C) pipe (D) sink (E) heart

3 **instrument → cello : species →**

(A) mammal (B) animal (C) predator (D) carnivore (E) koala

4 **typewriter → computer : sundial →**

(A) clock (B) sunglasses (C) number (D) time (E) thermometer

5 **emit → time : reviled →**

(A) remit (B) watch (C) deliver (D) revile (E) liver

6 **vertical → horizontal : increase →**

(A) rise (B) steady (C) decrease (D) parallel (E) perpendicular

7 **blocks → wall : thread →**

(A) loom (B) cloth (C) cotton (D) needle (E) wool

8 **hole → whole : sell →**

(A) cell (B) sold (C) lease (D) seal (E) price

9 **inch → foot : decade →**

(A) calendar (B) day (C) time (D) century (E) year

10 **translator → translation : judge →**

(A) ruling (B) jury (C) court (D) lawyer (E) production

11 **apprehensive → anxious : placid →**

(A) worried (B) liquid (C) volatile (D) kind (E) tranquil

12 **safe → valuables : silo →**

(A) farm (B) grain (C) tractor (D) box (E) cellar

13 **face → mask : candy →**

(A) sugar (B) sweet (C) calories (D) lollipop (E) wrapper

14 **mountain → summit : wave →**

(A) tsunami (B) crest (C) bottom (D) ocean (E) current

15 **authentic → fake : fair →**

(A) settlement (B) lenient (C) unjust (D) ordinary (E) realistic

16 **heat → burn : rain →**

(A) cloud (B) flood (C) drops (D) tornado (E) moisture

17 **size → shrink : light →**

(A) night (B) bulb (C) decrease (D) switch (E) dim

18 **opaque → transparent : contemporary →**

(A) artistic (B) realistic (C) modern (D) old-fashioned (E) equal

19 **dry → moisture : borderless →**

(A) boundary (B) open (C) area (D) town (E) path

20 **science → biology : mathematics →**

(A) chemistry (B) geometry (C) addition (D) geography (E) subject

Directions: The top 3 words go together in some way. Which answer choice goes best with the top words?

1 **Asian** **African** **North American**

Ⓐ Mexican Ⓑ Indian Ⓒ Continental Ⓓ European Ⓔ Spanish

2 **brain** **liver** **kidney**

Ⓐ blood Ⓑ eyebrow Ⓒ elbow Ⓓ hair Ⓔ intestines

3 **month** **century** **second**

Ⓐ decade Ⓑ daydream Ⓒ meter Ⓓ liter Ⓔ time

4 **ape** **monkey** **baboon**

Ⓐ horse Ⓑ squirrel Ⓒ gorilla Ⓓ giraffe Ⓔ lion

5 **scarlet** **cherry** **crimson**

Ⓐ gold Ⓑ bronze Ⓒ turquoise Ⓓ emerald Ⓔ ruby

6 **educate** **train** **coach**

Ⓐ produce Ⓑ instruct Ⓒ compute Ⓓ test Ⓔ compete

7 **dictionary** **biography** **textbook**

Ⓐ science fiction Ⓑ book Ⓒ encyclopedia Ⓓ author Ⓔ fairytale

8 **lane** **passage** **trail**

Ⓐ car Ⓑ speed Ⓒ GPS Ⓓ garage Ⓔ highway

9 **rise** **ascend** **mount**

Ⓐ balance Ⓑ support Ⓒ steady Ⓓ soar Ⓔ descend

10 **astounded** **stunned** **astonished**

Ⓐ aware Ⓑ energetic Ⓒ amazed Ⓓ excited Ⓔ impatient

11 **arid** **parched** **wilted**

(A) dehydrated (B) moisture (C) soggy (D) sandy (E) drenched

12 **opposite** **antonym** **unlike**

(A) parallel (B) similar (C) contrary (D) choice (E) odd

13 **firefighter** **police officer** **paramedic**

(A) reporter (B) electrician (C) tutor (D) lifeguard (E) trucker

14 **bottom** **foot** **foundation**

(A) building (B) base (C) first (D) strength (E) introduction

15 **forecast** **foretell** **project**

(A) predict (B) read (C) explain (D) teleport (E) travel

16 **fatigued** **exhausted** **weary**

(A) snooze (B) energetic (C) recovered (D) infected (E) drowsy

17 **ally** **supporter** **teammate**

(A) announcer (B) referee (C) partner (D) spectator (E) player

18 **Amazon** **Mississippi** **Rio Grande**

(A) London (B) New York (C) Nile (D) Florida (E) France

19 **warehouse** **garage** **hangar**

(A) vault (B) highway (C) tractor (D) concrete (E) vehicle

20 **alphabetical** **chronological** **geographical**

(A) classical (B) comical (C) digital (D) numerical (E) skeptical

18/20

Directions: There is a missing word in the sentence. Which answer choice would go best in the sentence?

1 **Unfortunately, this passport has expired and is no longer ___.**

(A) legible (B) valid (C) broken (D) limited (E) void

2 **We doubted that the contestant's claim was ____ because it is practically impossible to run 200 miles in a single day.**

(A) accelerated (B) swift (C) unreliable (D) credible (E) dishonest

3 **I expect the price of the car will probably ____ by the end of the year, so I plan to wait and buy it then.**

(A) intensify (B) reject (C) inflate (D) increase (E) decrease

4 **A thorough investigation of the suspects certainly has the potential to ____ who committed the crime.**

(A) reveal (B) conceal (C) disguise (D) continue (E) perpetuate

5 **The author describes the party in such ____ detail, that it enables readers to practically experience the celebration for themselves.**

(A) incorrect (B) inaccurate (C) meticulous (D) bland (E) ordinary

6 The investigator ____ that the bank robber also stole a car, although she has not provided evidence of that yet.

(A) alleges (B) magnifies (C) congratulates (D) arrests (E) depends

7 His agreement to purchase the house is ____ on the roof being repaired.

(A) entirety (B) conditional (C) absolute (D) independent (E) contrary

8 The main ____ that will determine the location of our next vacation is the price of airline tickets.

(A) holiday (B) setting (C) address (D) factor (E) speed

9 The ____ for the "perfect attendance" award is not missing a single day of school.

(A) journal (B) assembly (C) dismissal (D) denial (E) criteria

10 Our most recent experiment results do not ____ with those of our previous experiments, as there is almost no connection between the two.

(A) correlate (B) divide (C) alter (D) change (E) conclude

11 **Their strategy to win the battle is to ____ their enemy on the island by destroying all bridges connecting to the mainland.**

(A) combine (B) unite (C) surrender (D) accept (E) isolate

12 **The plan is to ____ the shed into a greenhouse by replacing the wooden walls and roof with glass.**

(A) destroy (B) convert (C) demolish (D) replace (E) duplicate

13 **My mother's perfume has such a ____ scent that we always know when she is nearby.**

(A) limited (B) moderate (C) distinct (D) vague (E) mild

14 **Our ____ for sorting waste had to be ____ when the recycling center informed us that plastic waste would no longer be accepted.**

(A) debris, protected (B) action, closed (C) procedure, curated (D) method, modified (E) process, artificial

15 **He didn't say so directly, but with the expression on his face, my father ____ that he didn't believe the salesperson's ____ claim that the new car would last 100 years.**

(A) stated, reduced (B) implied, exaggerated (C) shouted, elaborate (D) bellowed, inflated (E) whispered, modest

16 The lack of clean air is the most important ___ of the problem, so ___ that paragraph by underlining it in your report.

(A) objective, summarize
(B) solution, reduce
(C) theory, diminish
(D) aspect, emphasize
(E) idea, minimize

17 The concrete ____ where we keep the secret technology is quite ____, thanks to guards and an electric fence.

(A) barrier, towering
(B) structure, secure
(C) area, elevated
(D) construction, vulnerable
(E) building unprotected

18 The recipe calls for a ____ amount of salt, and if you only add an ____ amount, the dessert will not taste good.

(A) spicy, incorrect
(B) false, evaluated
(C) delicious, inaccurate
(D) random, estimated
(E) precise, approximate

19 The stomach virus is easily ____ from person to person, and if you don't wash your hands you'll be more ____ to getting sick.

(A) measured, connected
(B) bonded, cleared
(C) transmitted, susceptible
(D) transferred, secured
(E) received, immune

20 As we ____ the flower garden, he began to ____ signs of fear due to his phobia of butterflies.

(A) approached, exhibit
(B) exited, welcome
(C) enjoyed, persuade
(D) criticized, acclaim
(E) wandered, implant

Directions: Which choice makes the second set of pictures go together in the same way as the first set?

1

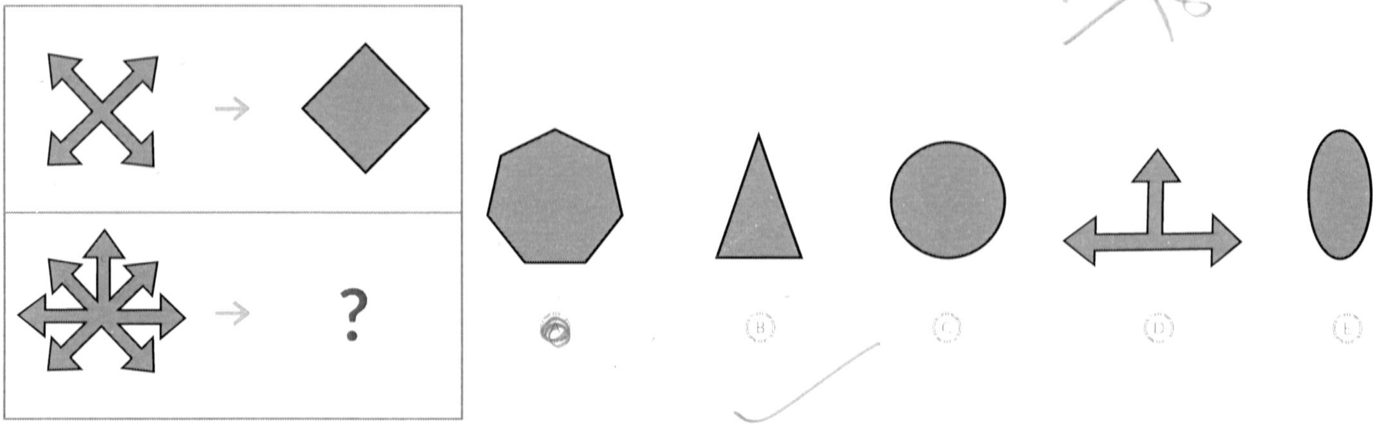

2

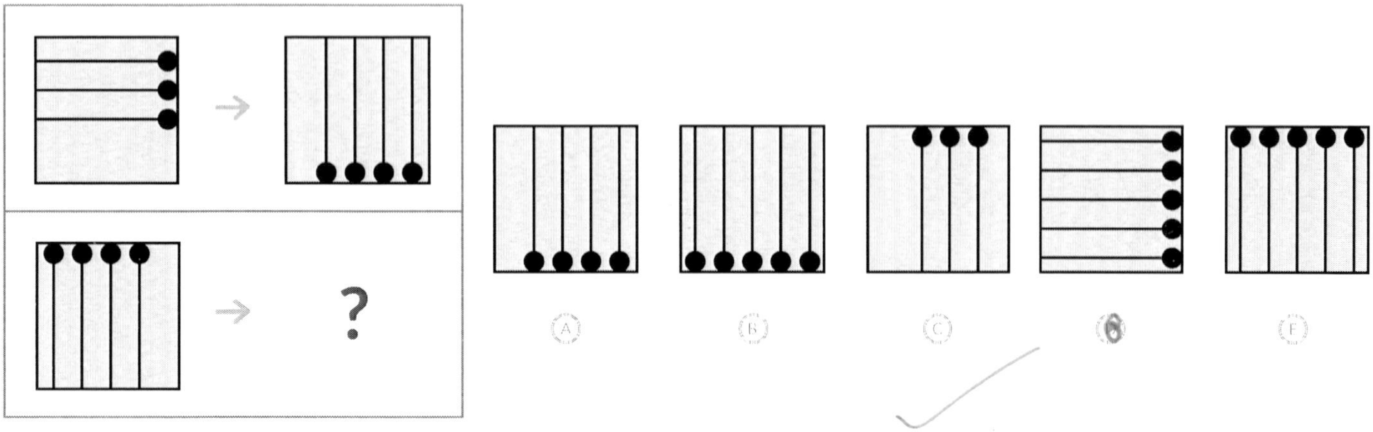

3

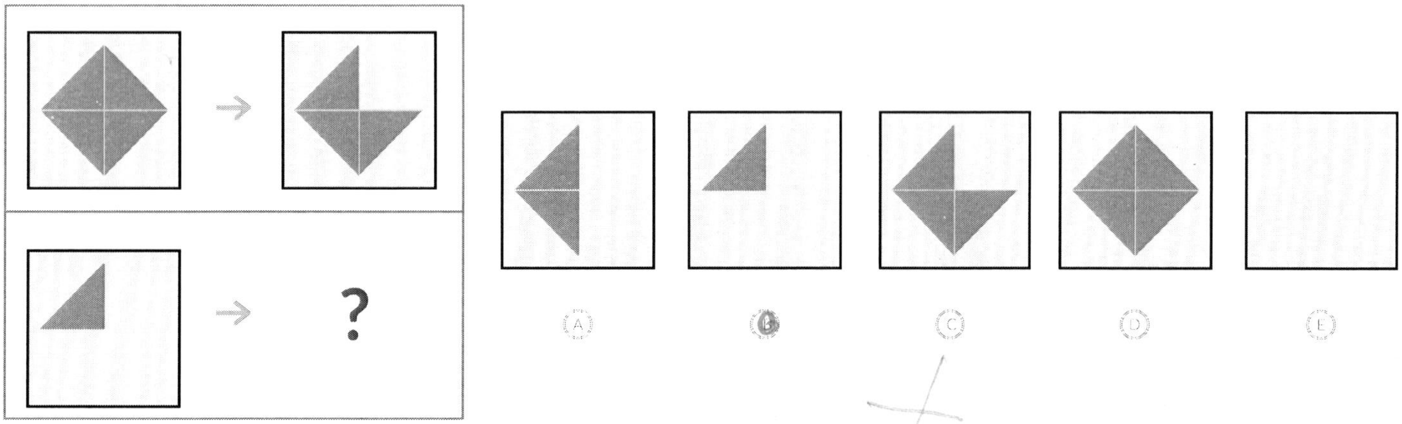

4

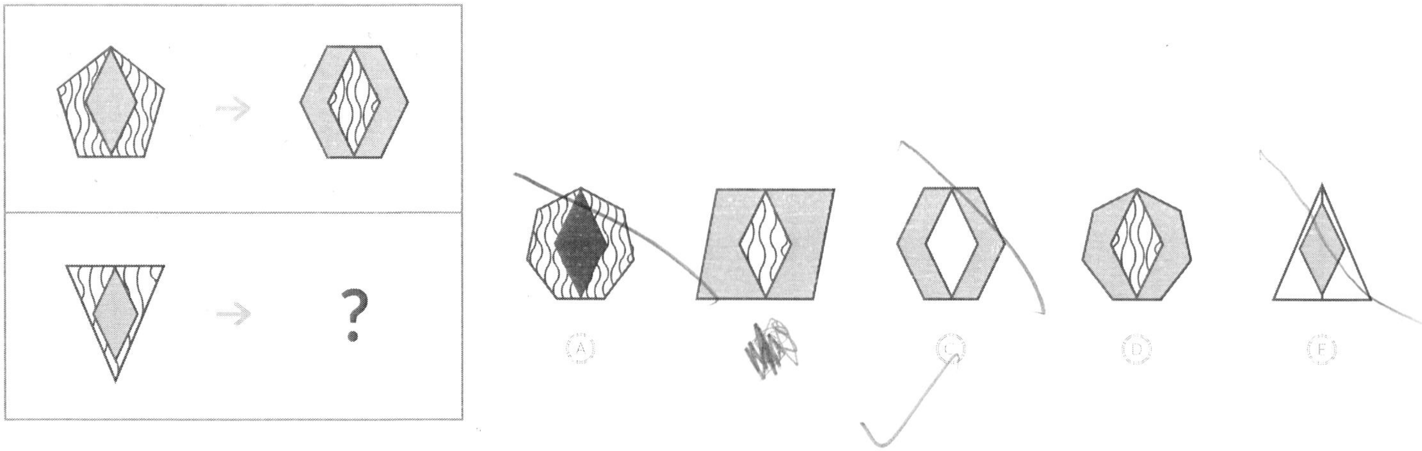

5

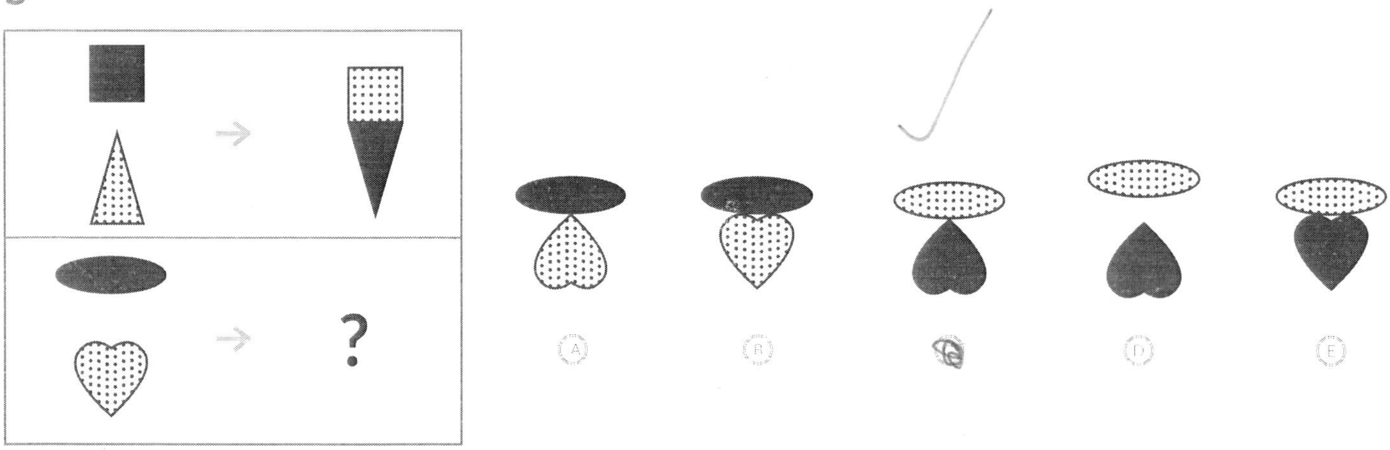

6

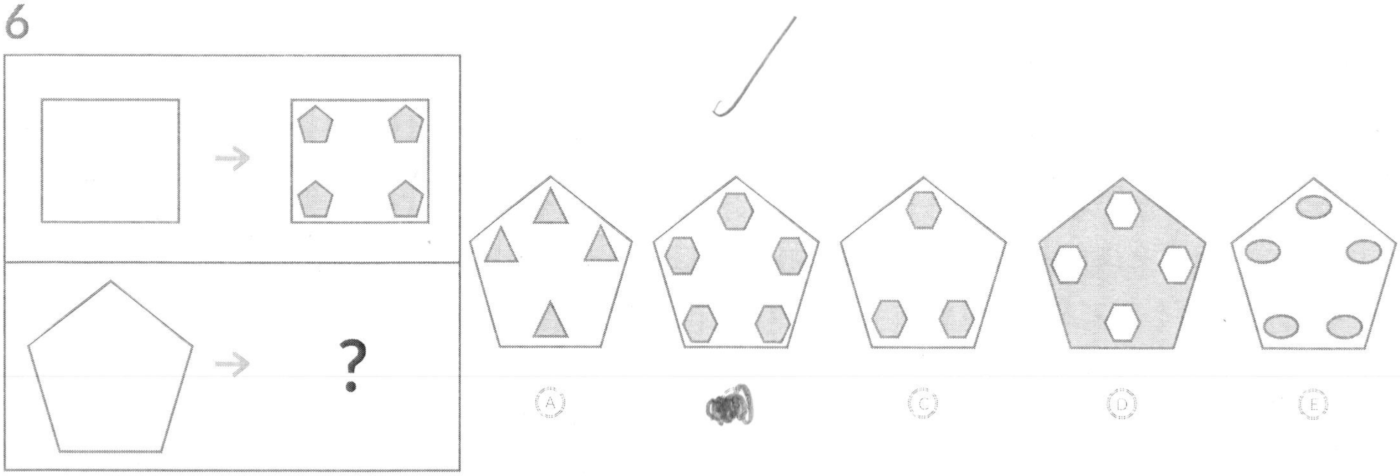

7

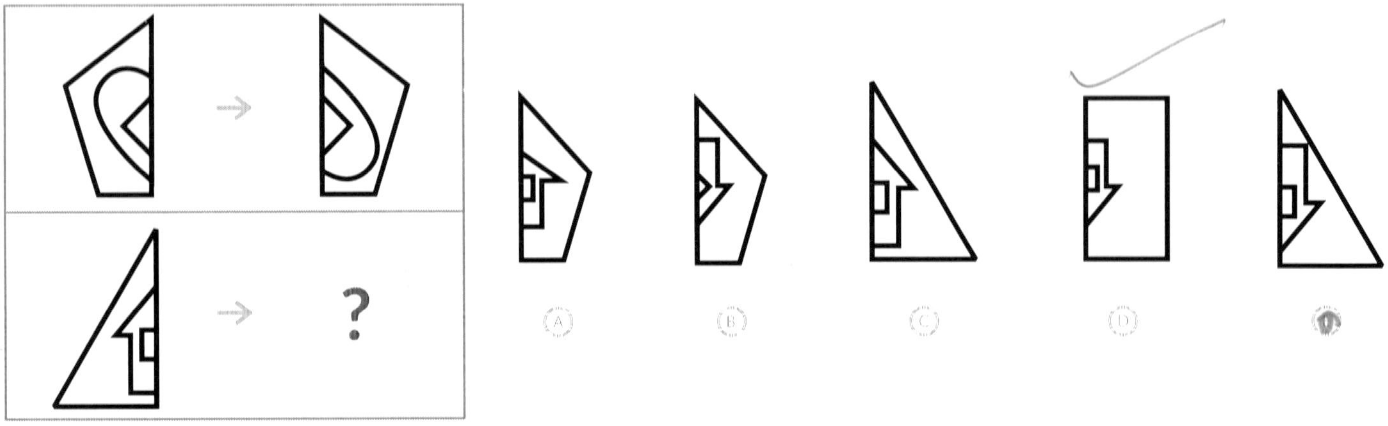

8

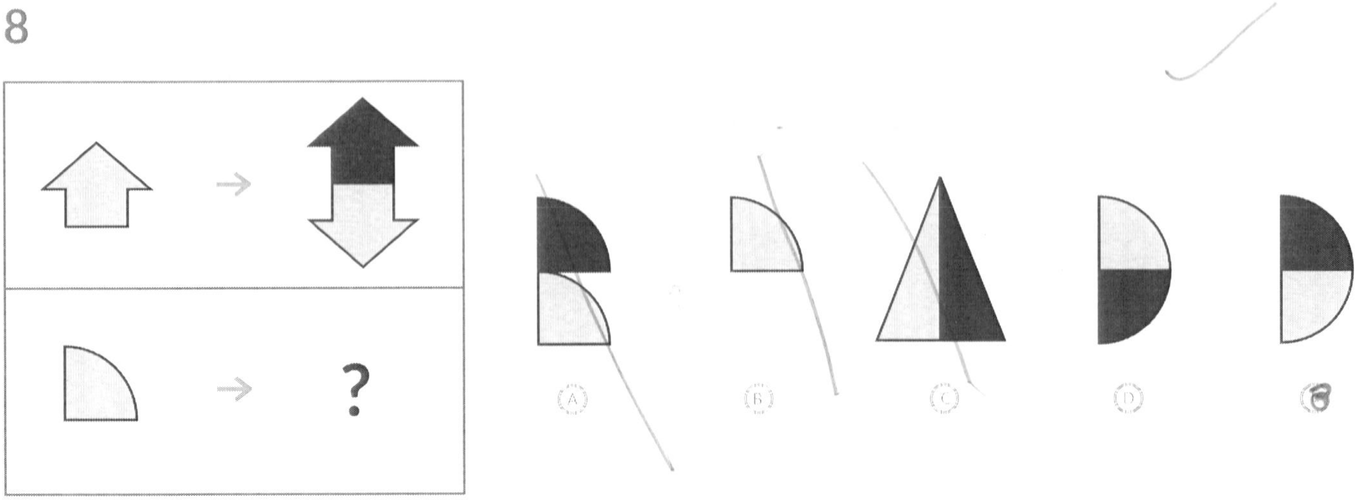

9

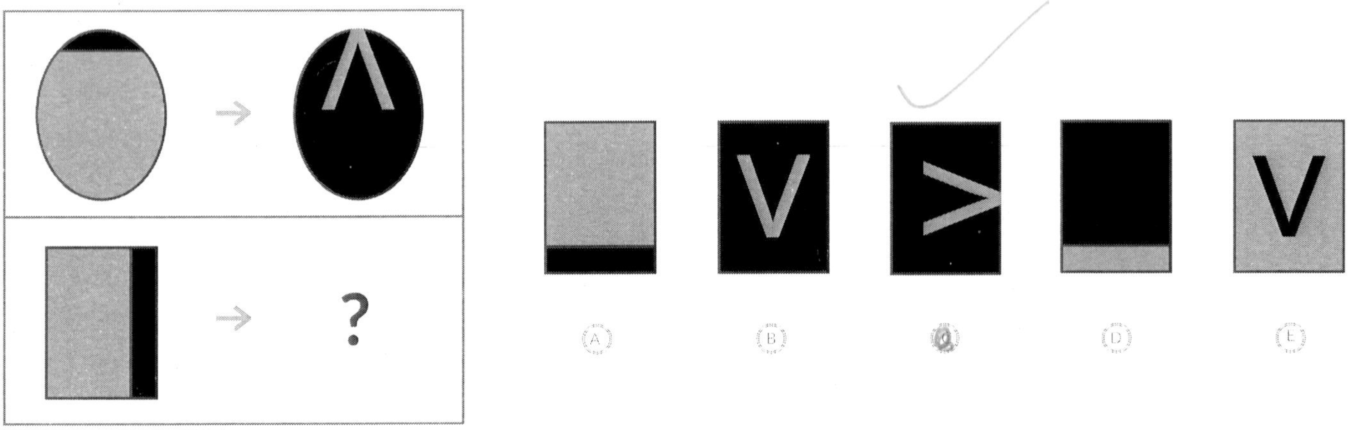

10

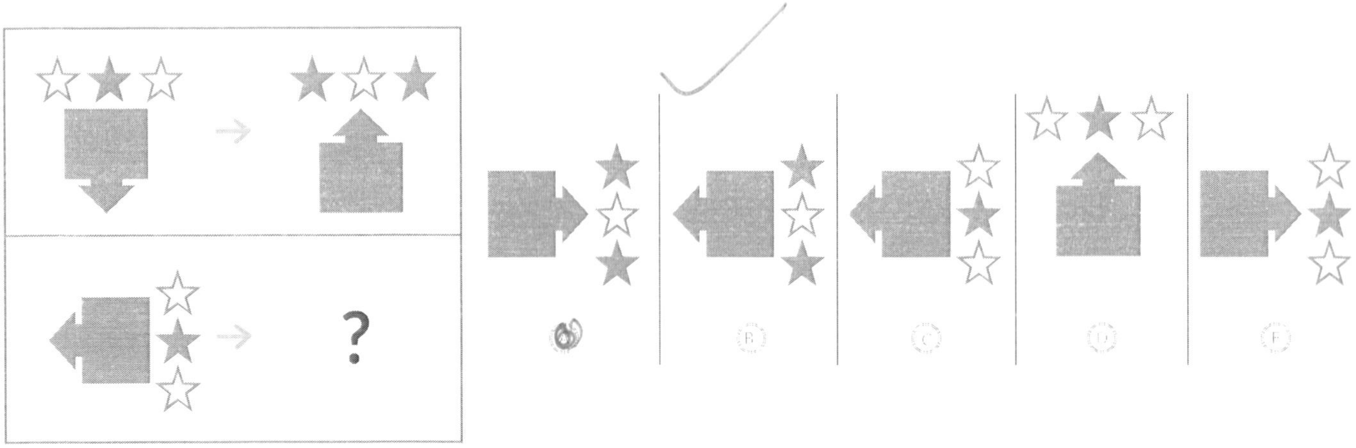

11

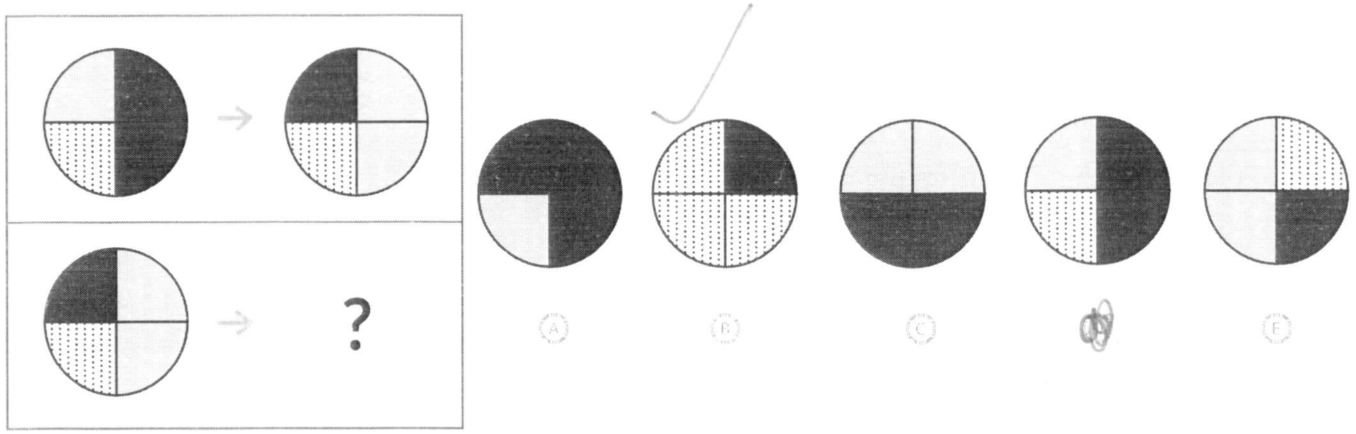

12

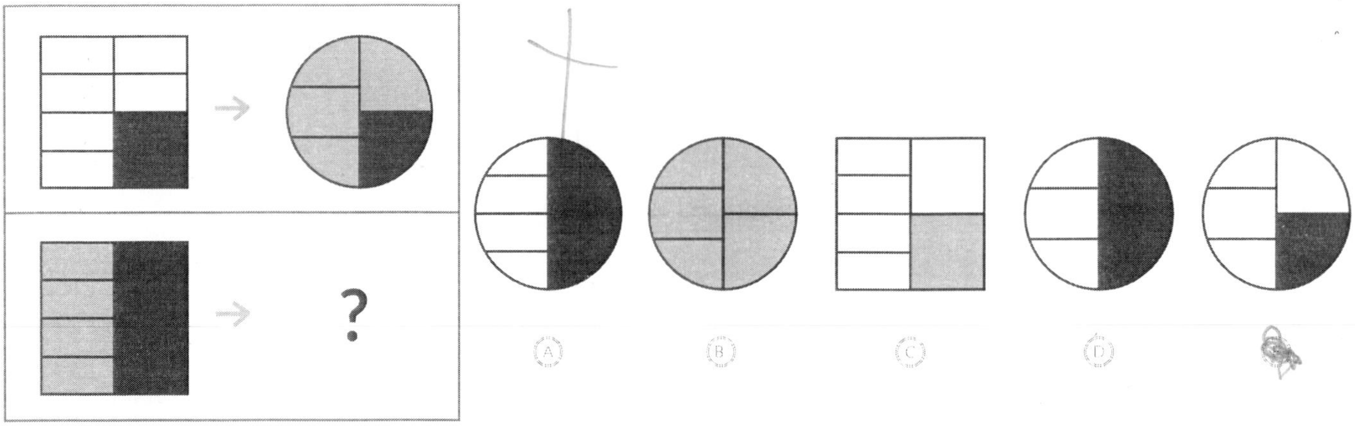

13

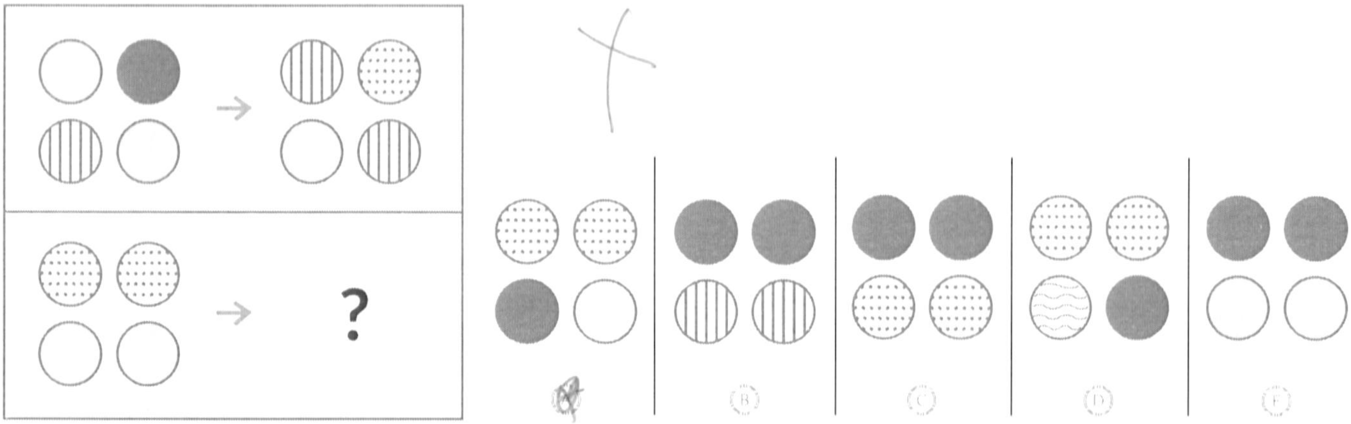

14

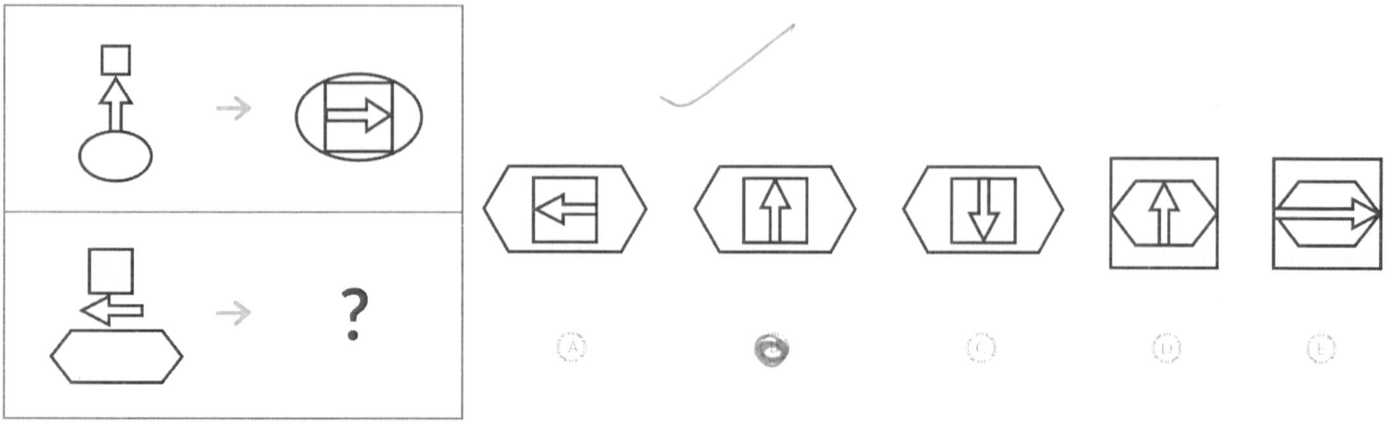

15

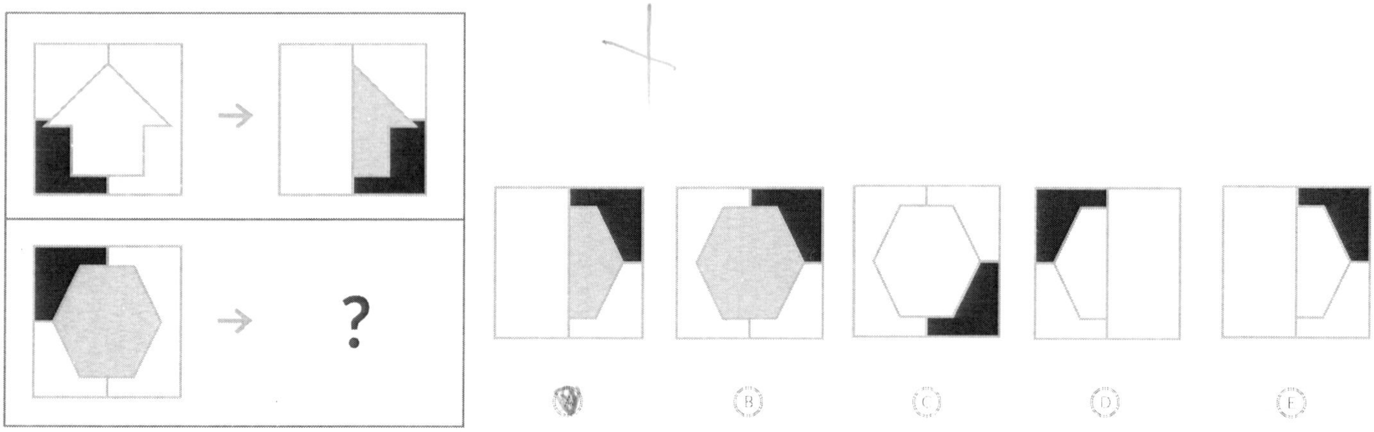

16

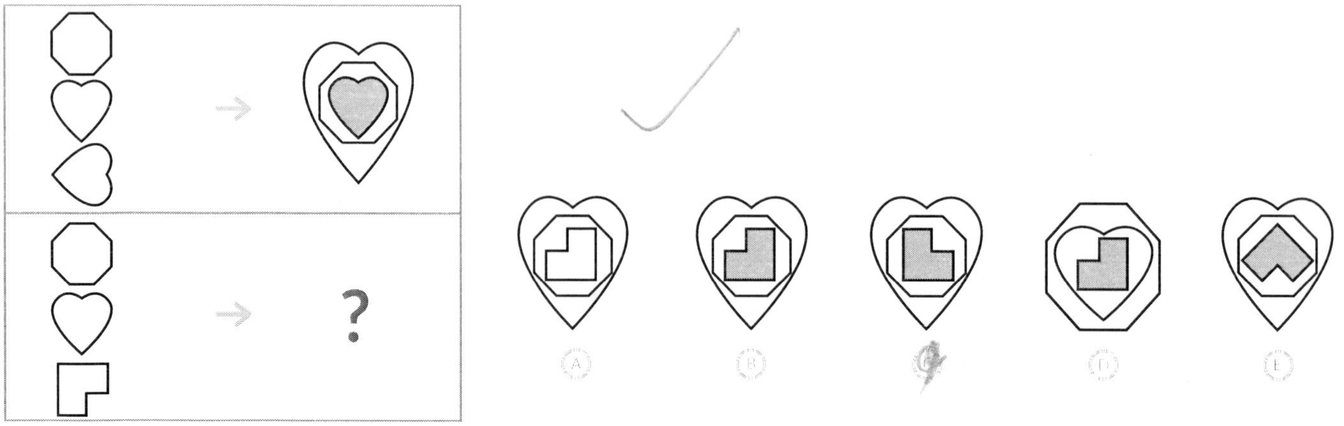

17

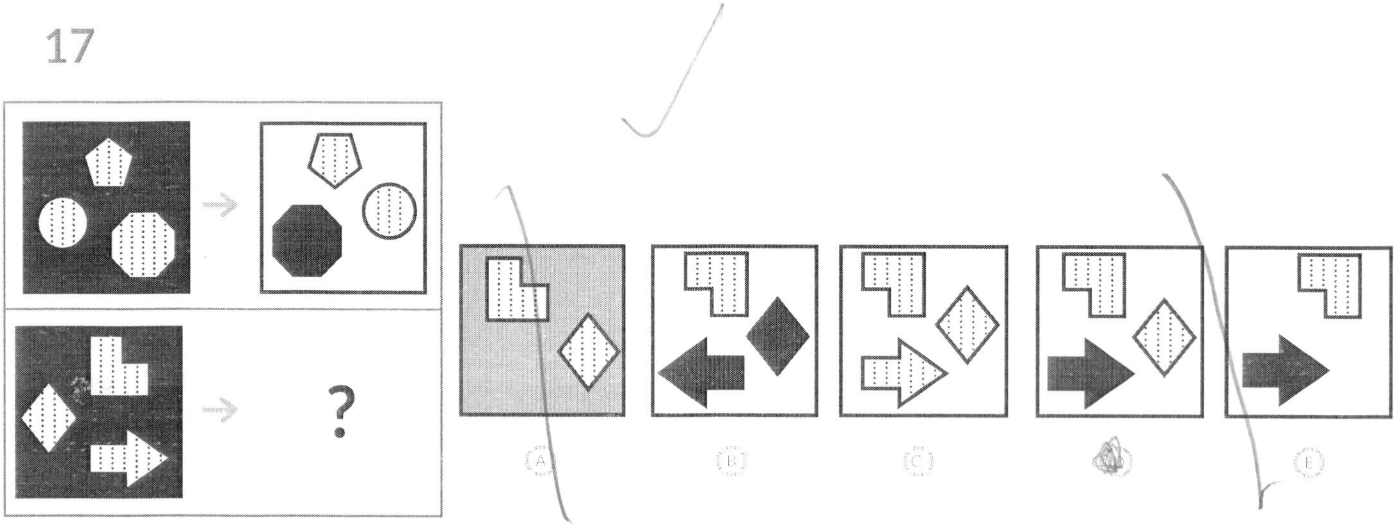

18

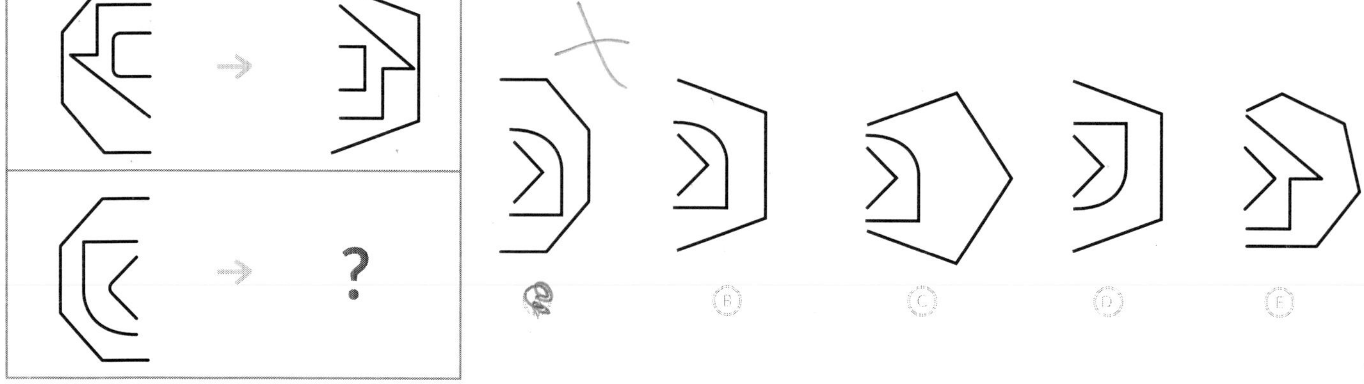

Directions: Which answer choice in the bottom row goes best with the 3 pictures in the top row?

1

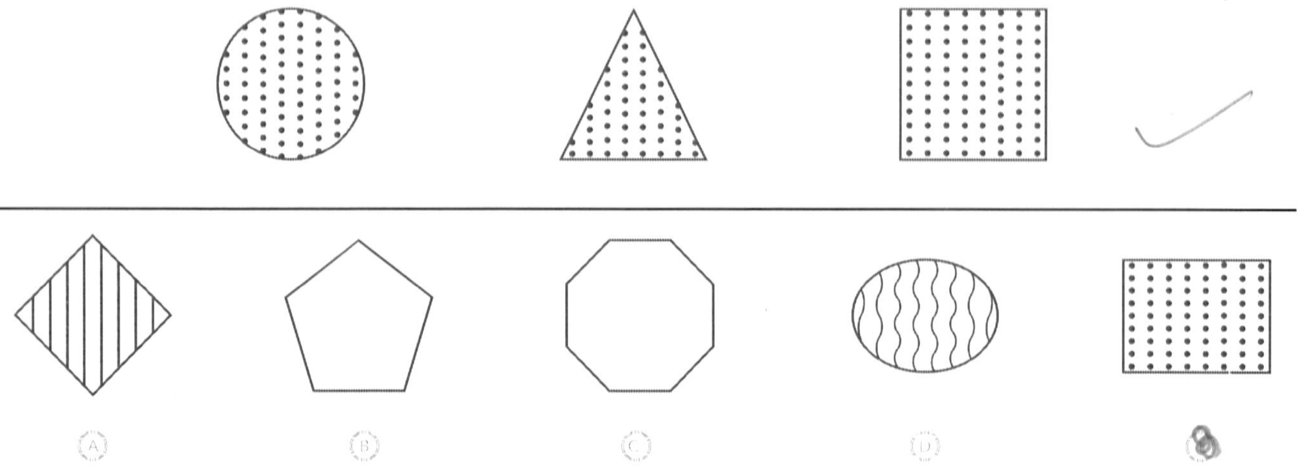

2

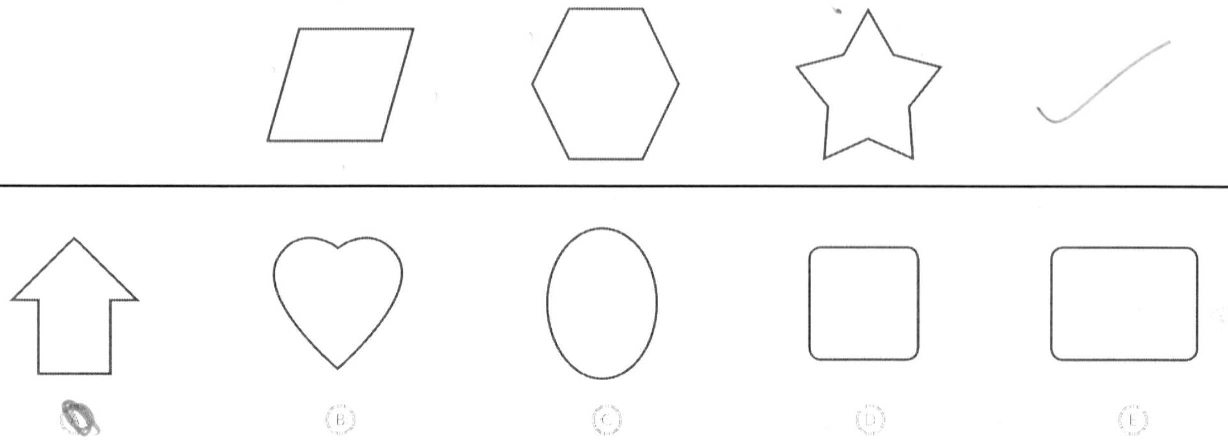

3

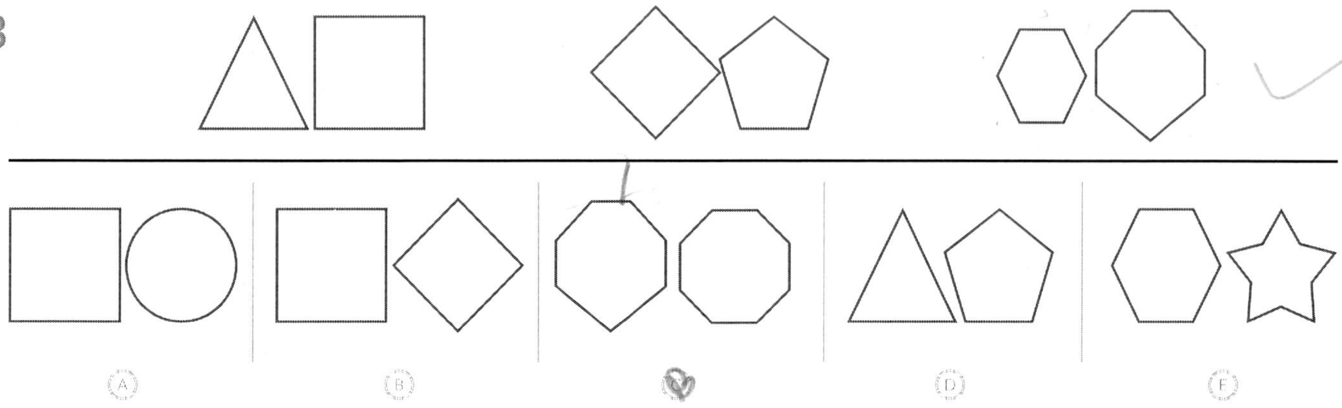

4

A B C D E

5

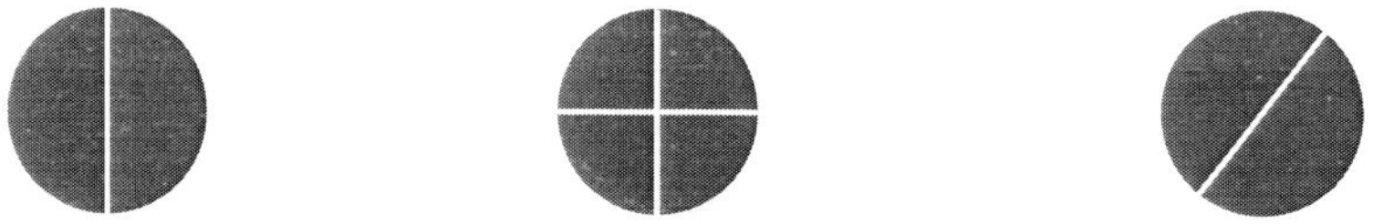

A B C D E

6

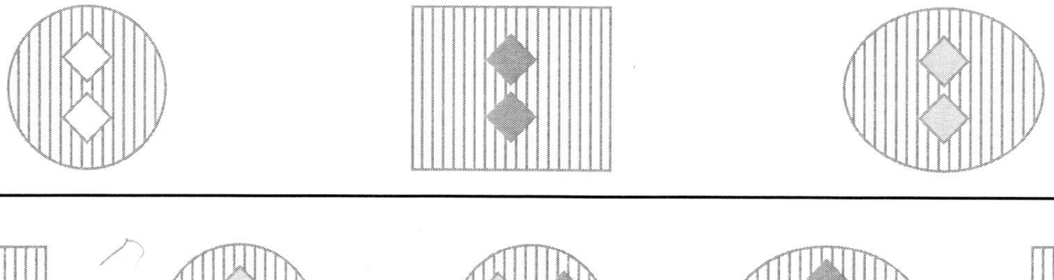

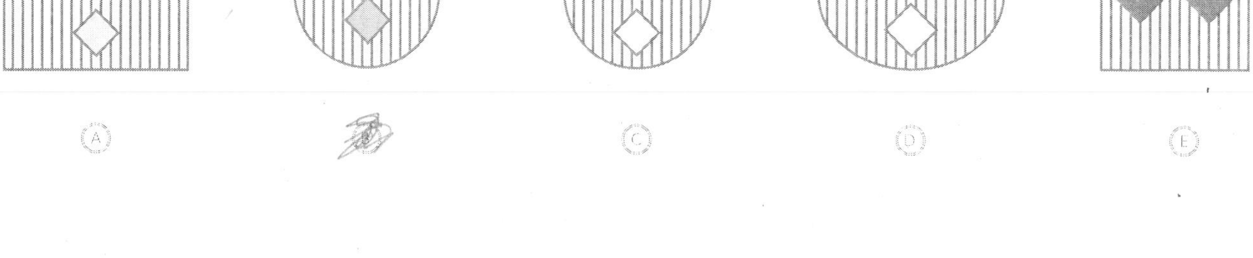

A B C D E

7

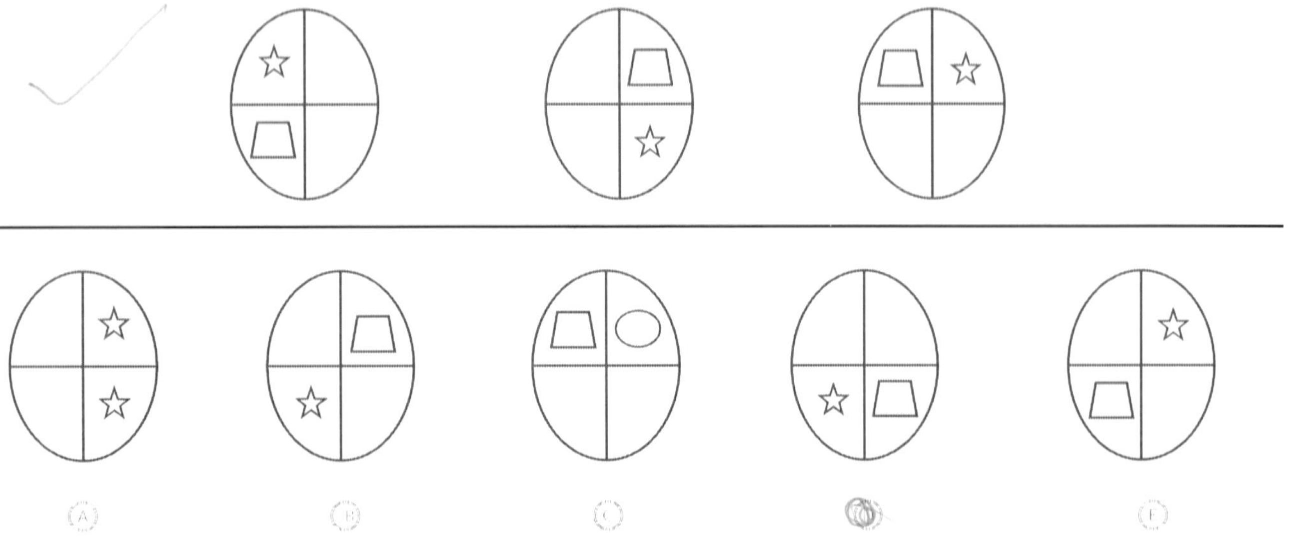

8

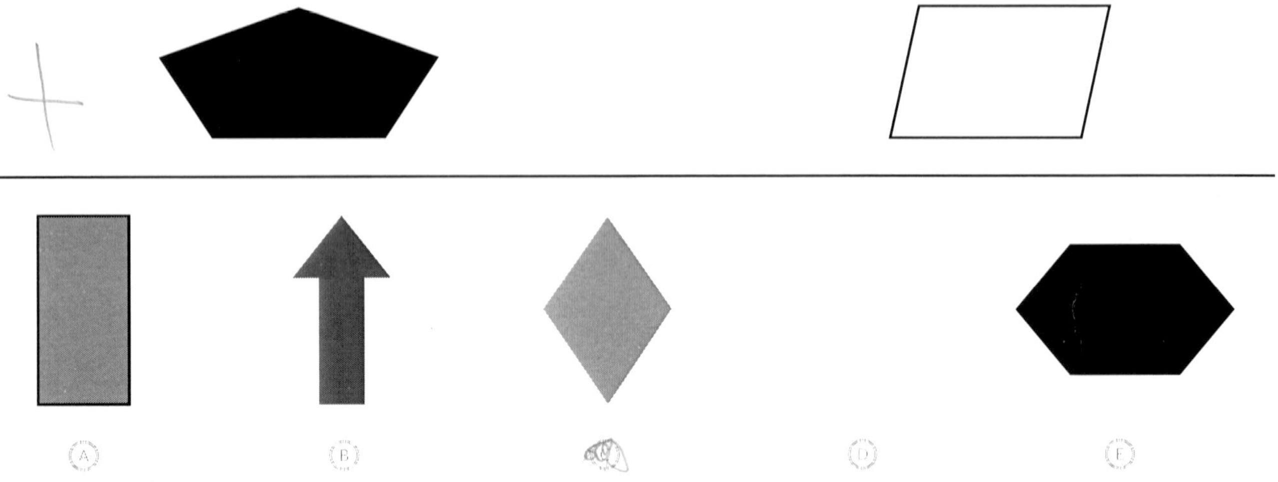

9

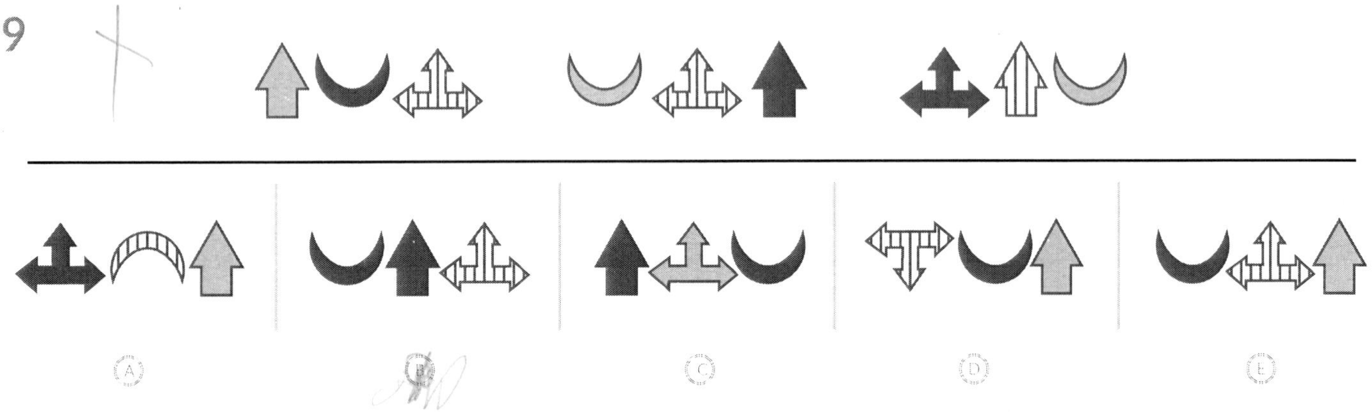

10

A B C D E

11

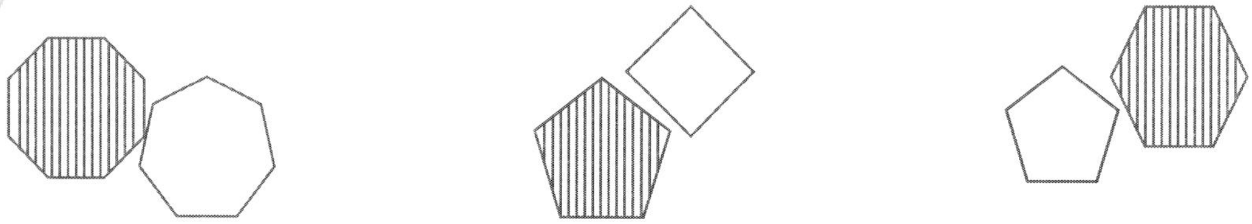

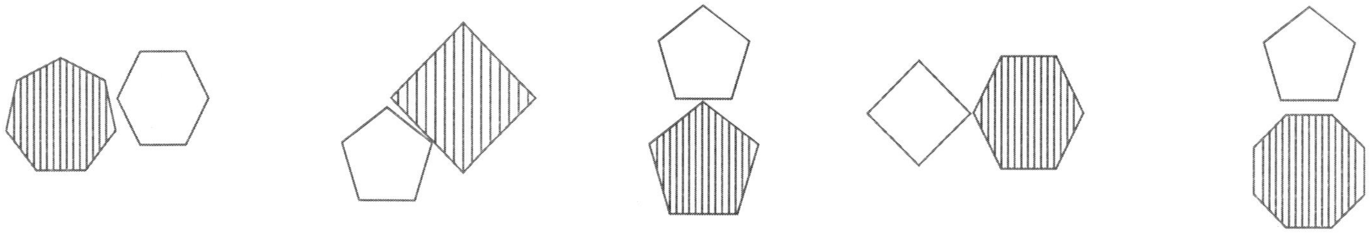

A B C D E

12

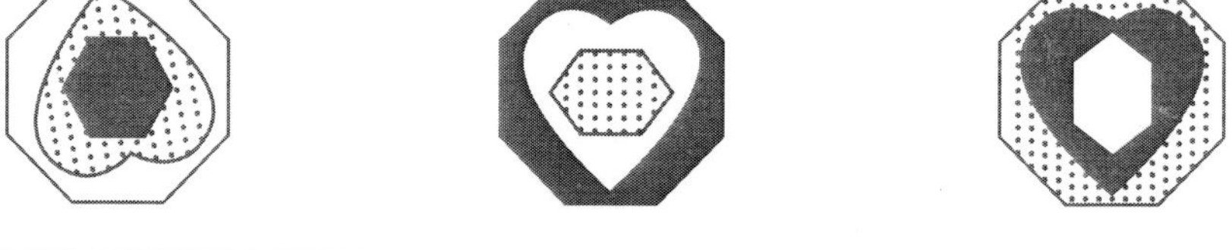

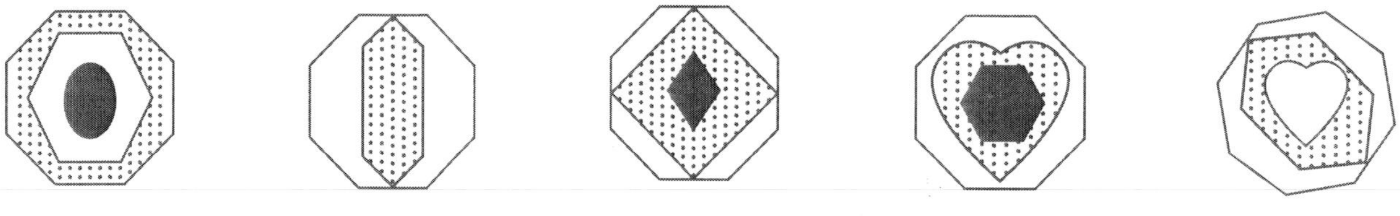

A B C D E

13

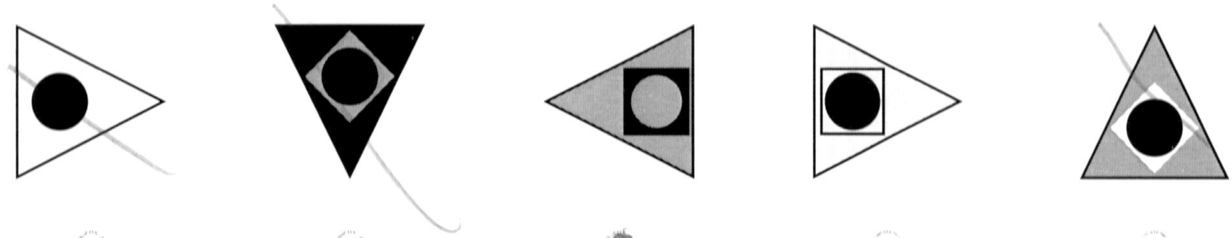

A B C D E

14

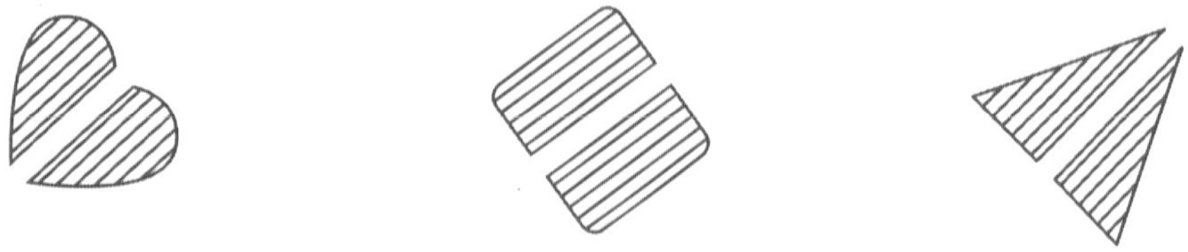

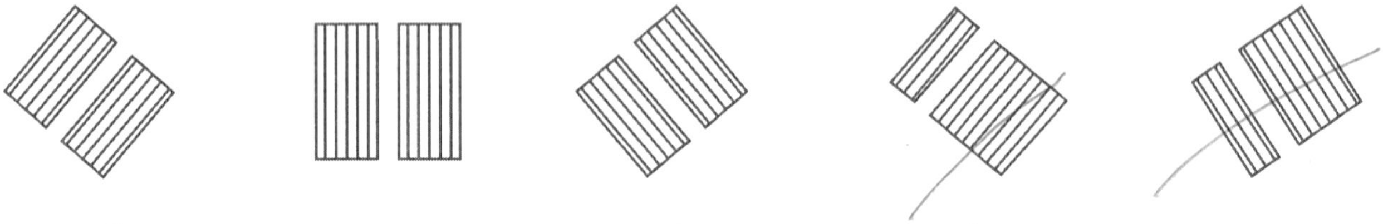

A B C D E

15

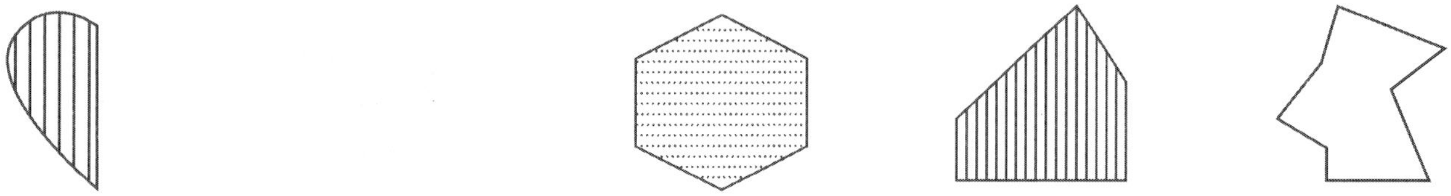

A B C D E

16

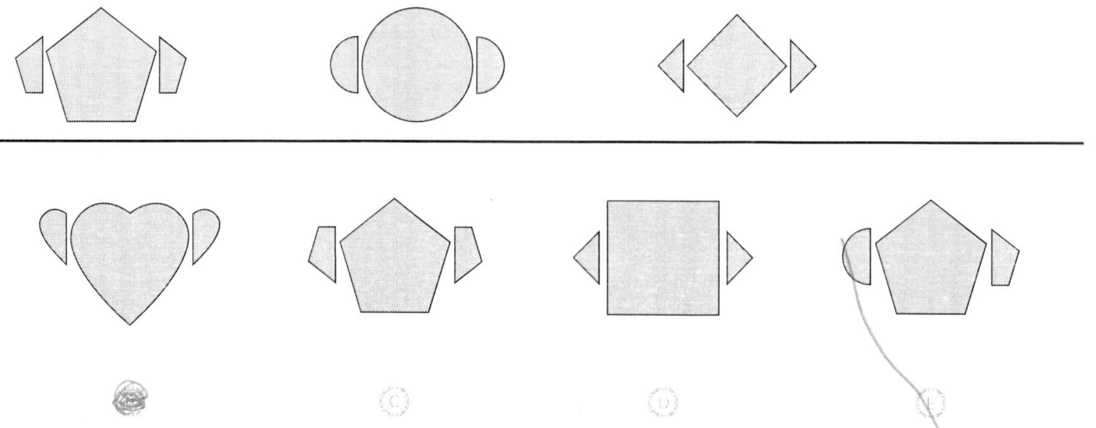

17

18

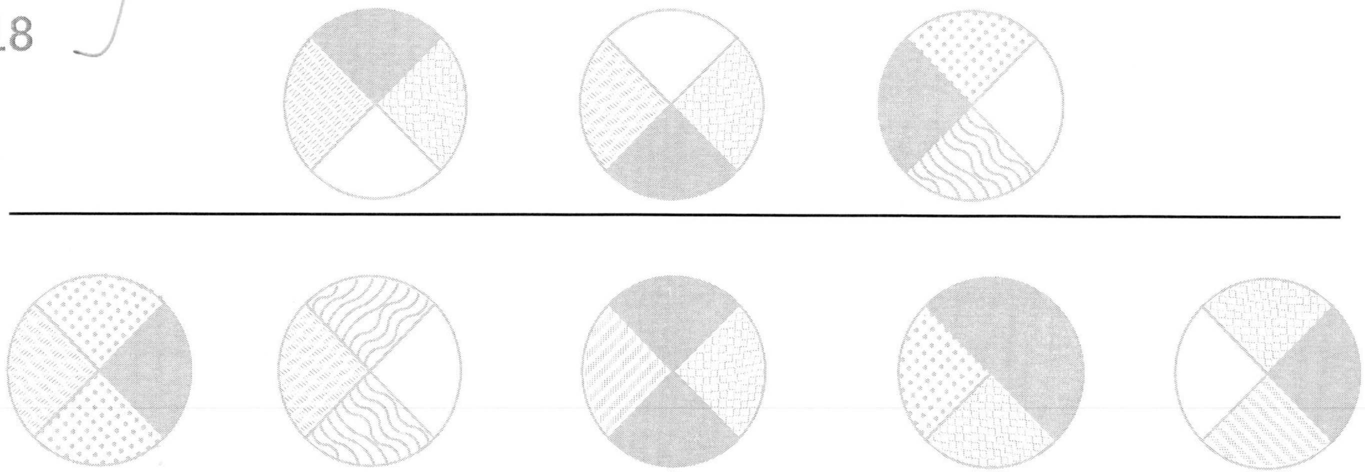

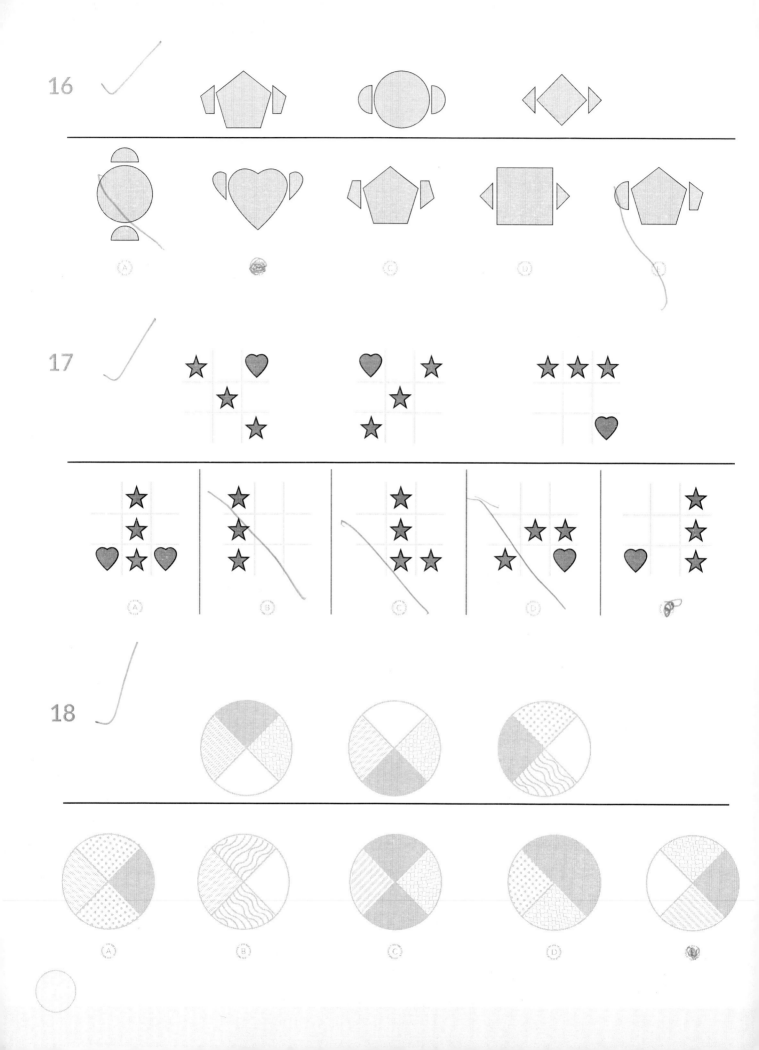

Directions: The top row shows a sheet of paper, how it was folded, and how holes were made in it. Which picture on the bottom row shows how the paper would look unfolded?

1

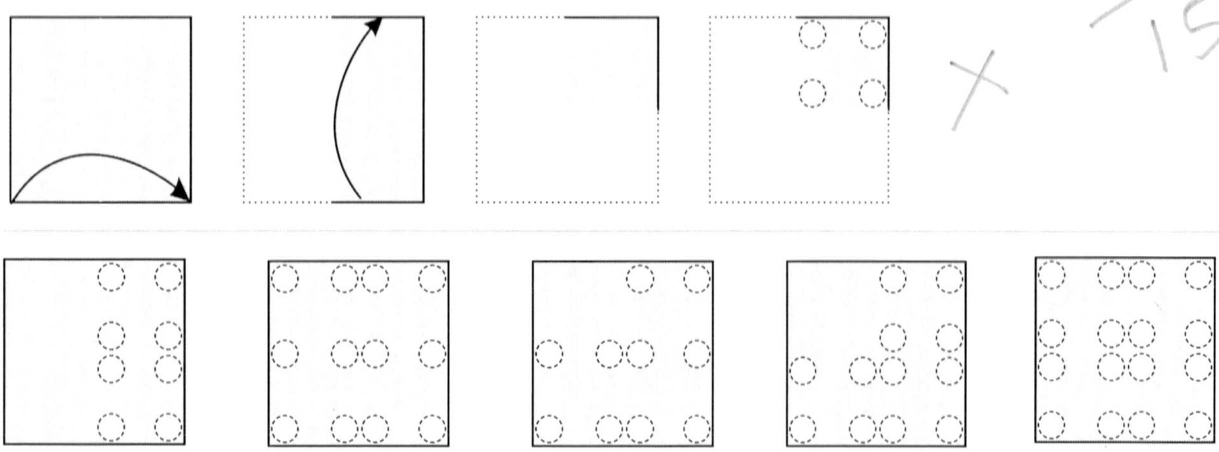

(A) (B) (C) (D) (E)

2

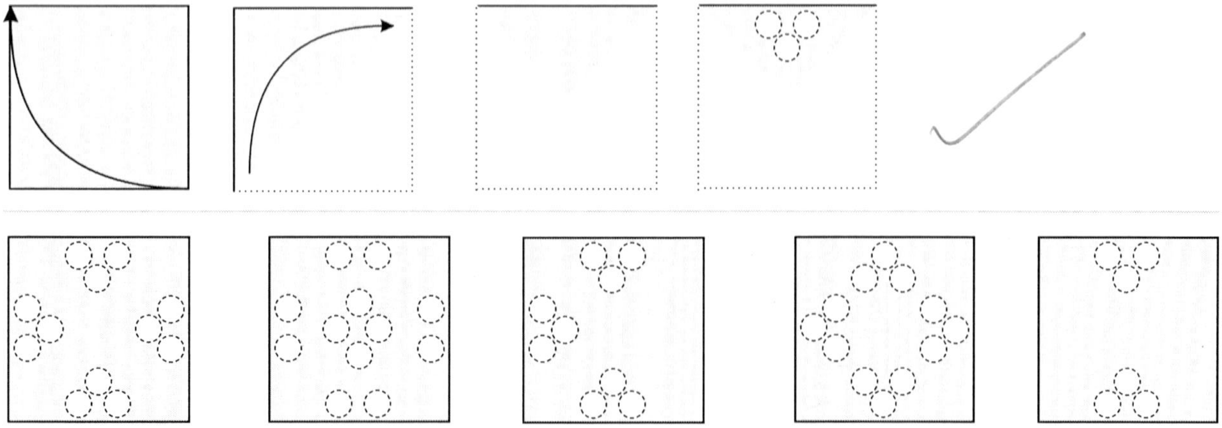

(A) (B) (C) (D) (E)

3

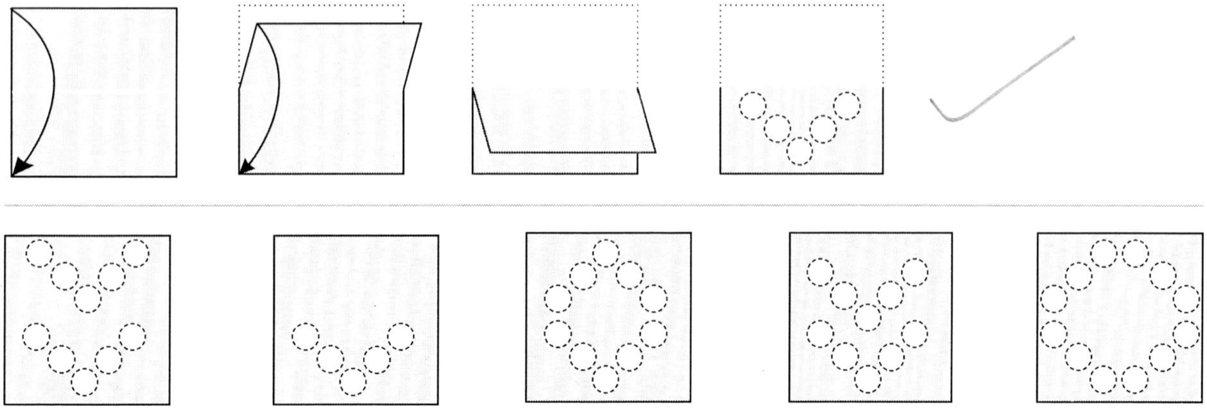

(A) (B) (C) (D) (E)

4

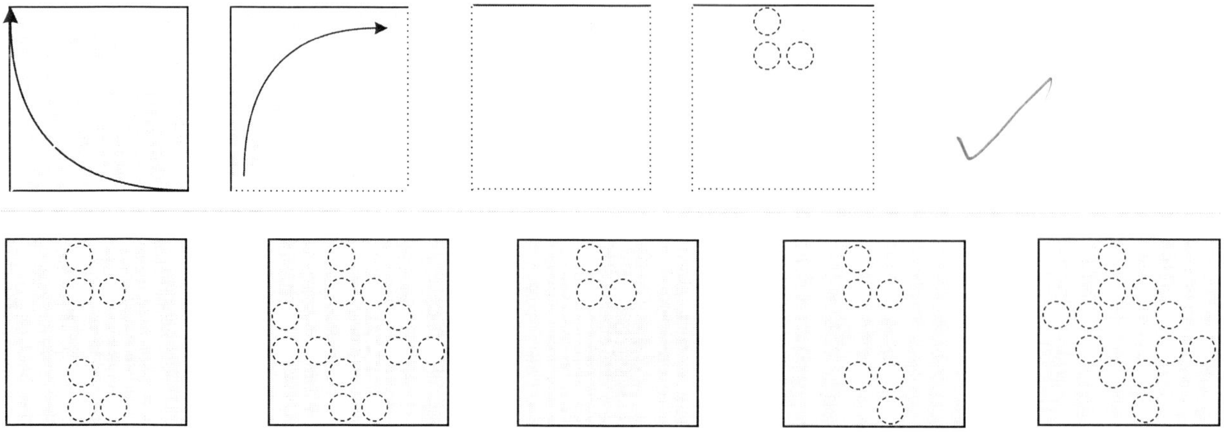

A B C D E

5

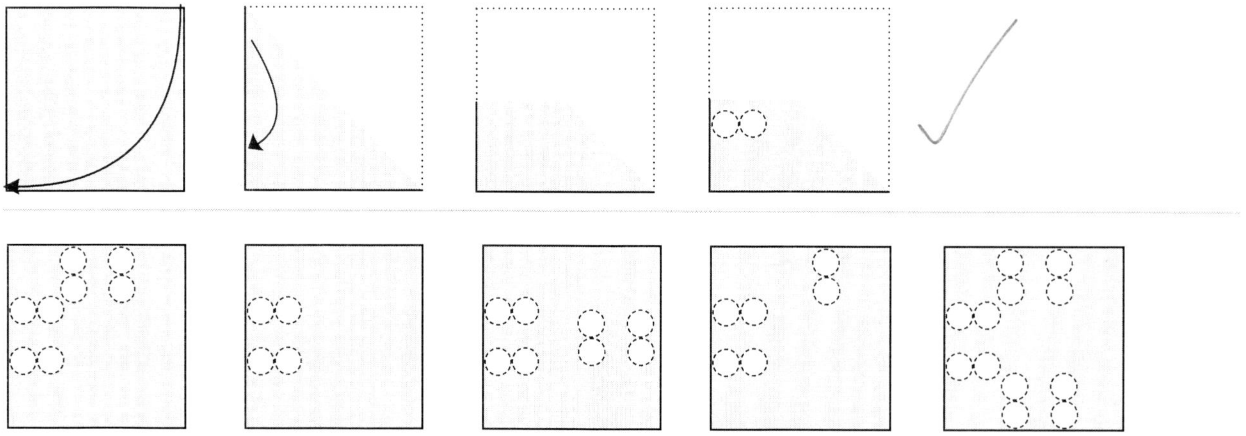

A B C D E

6

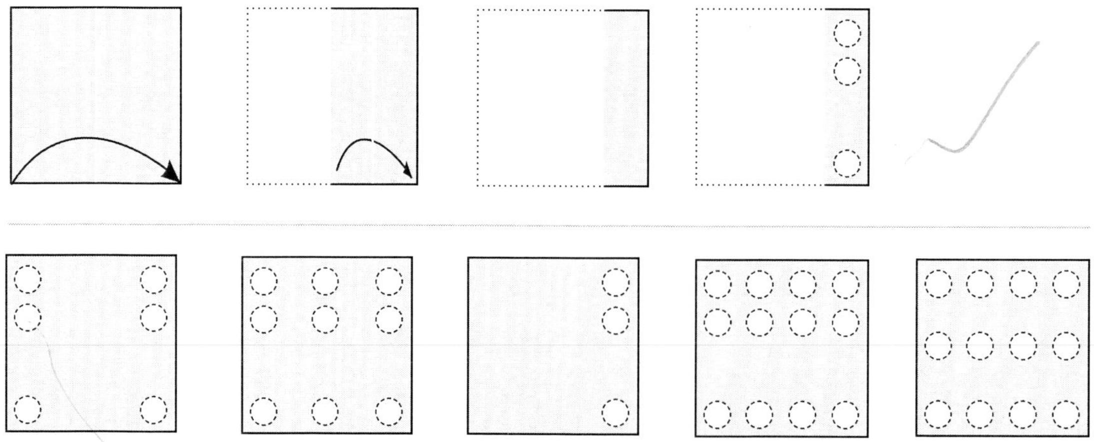

A B C D E

7

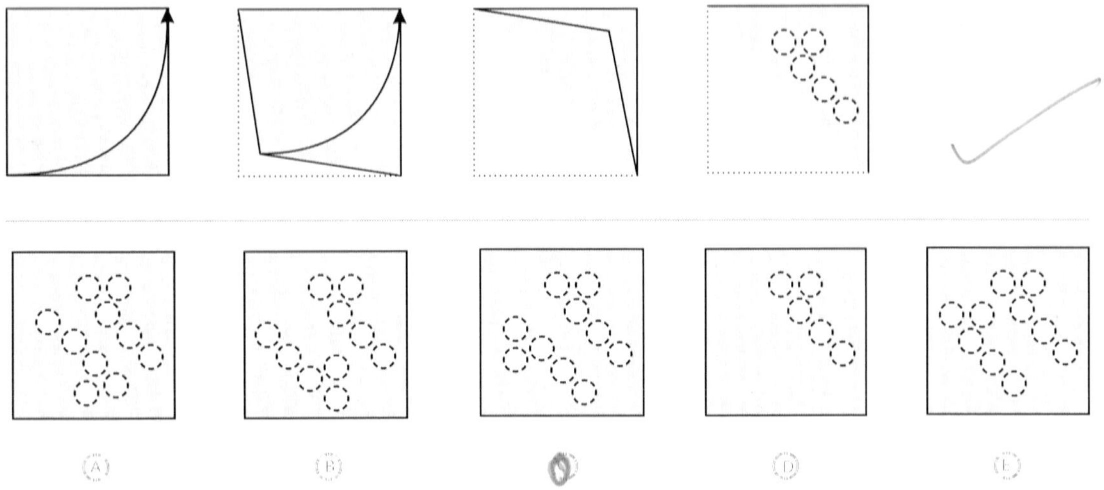

8

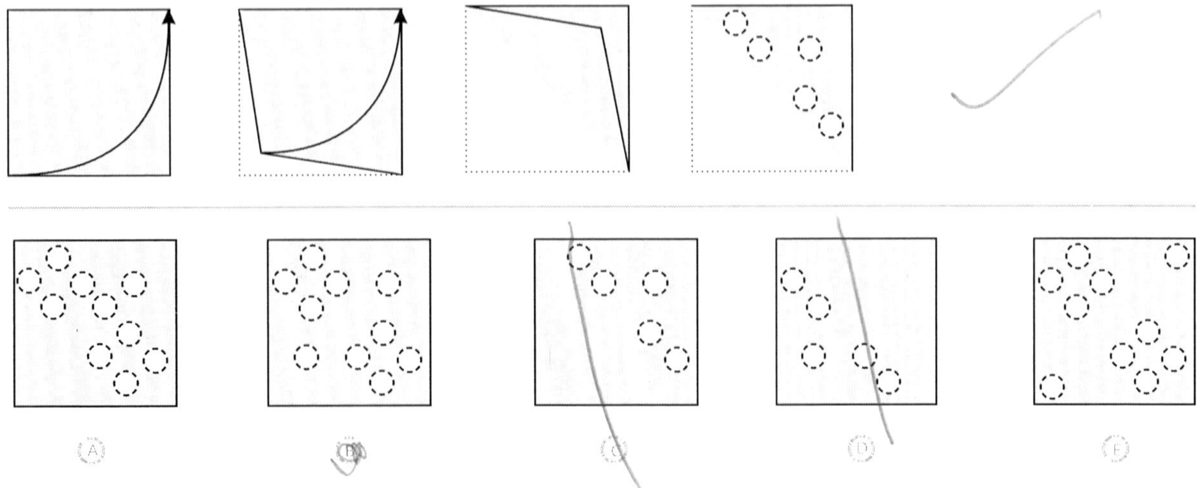

9

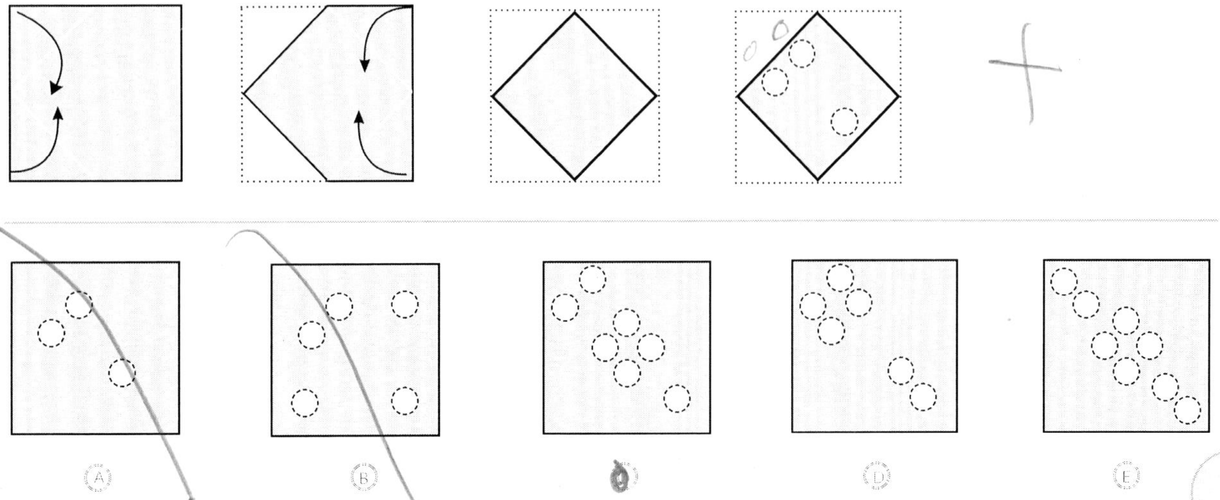

10

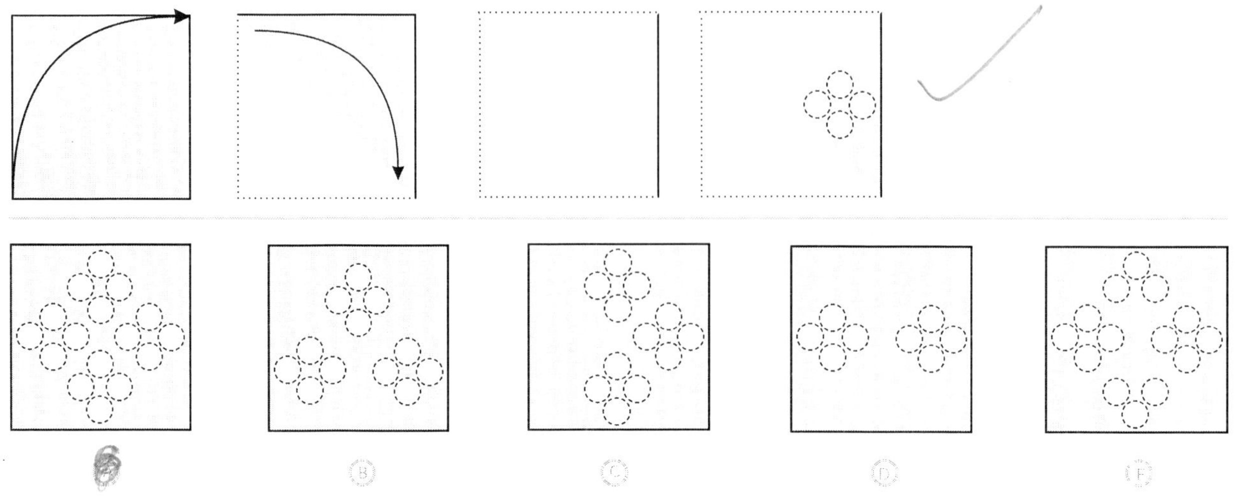

11

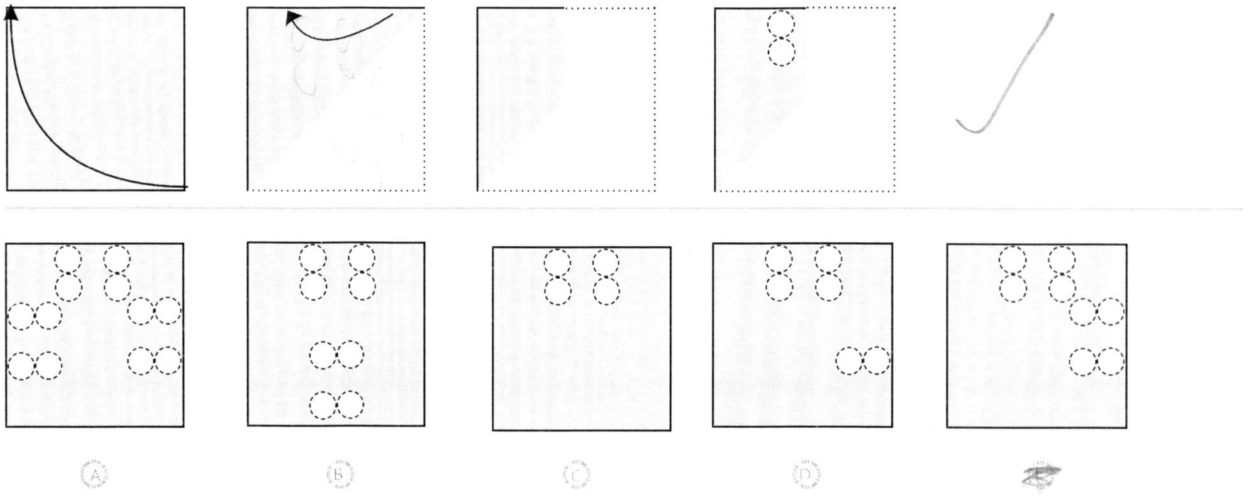

12

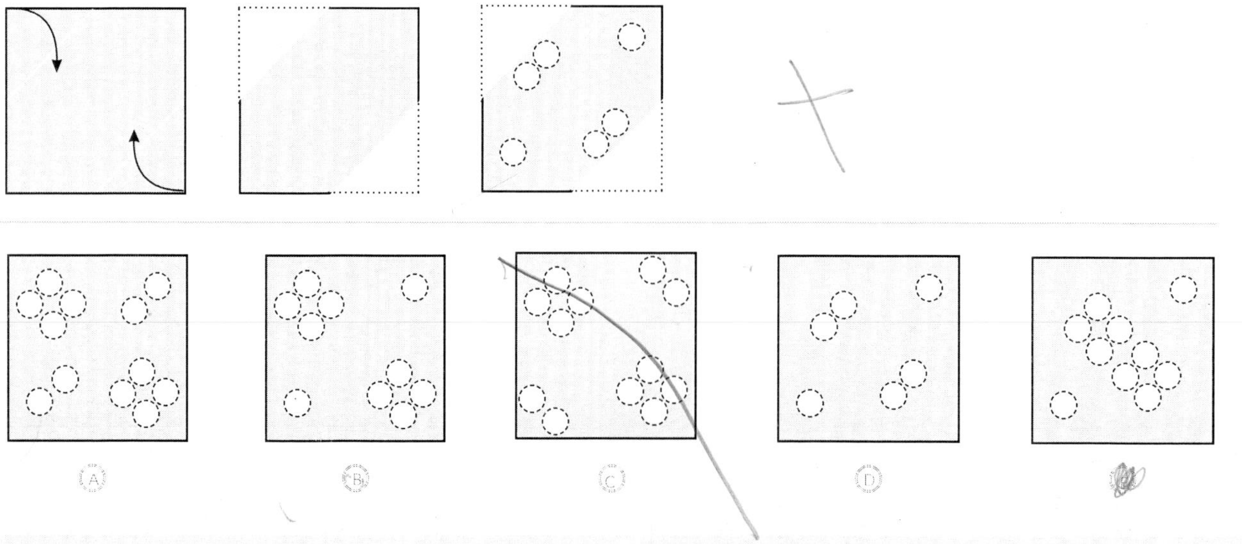

13

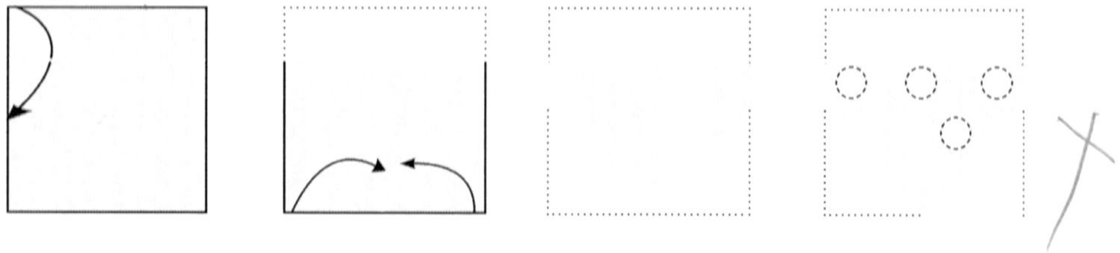

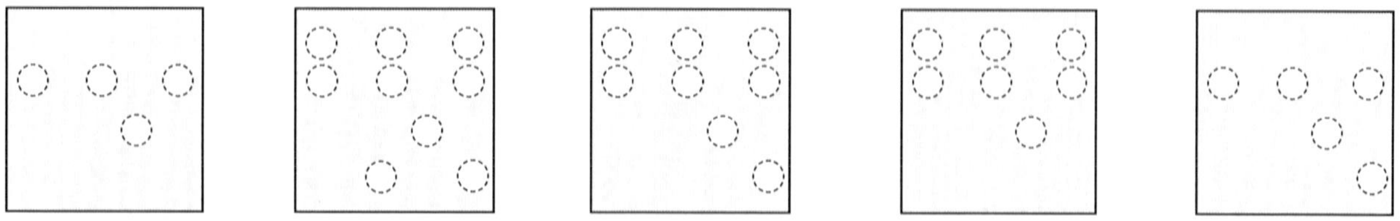

A B C D E

14

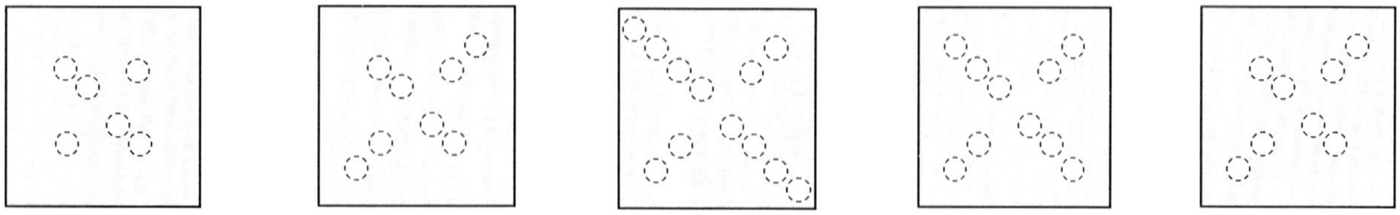

A B C D E

15

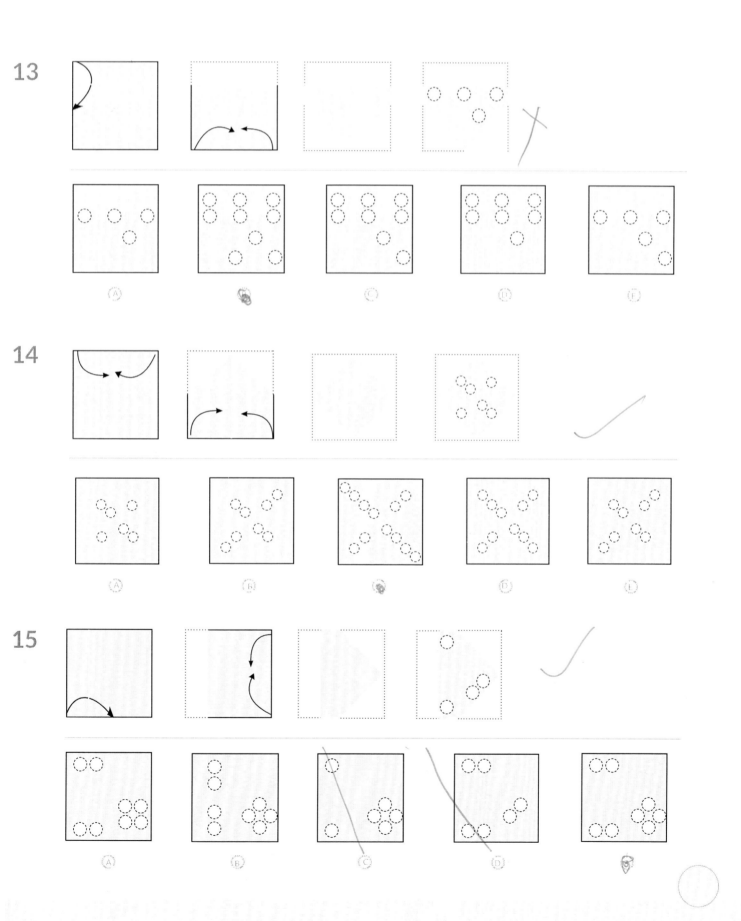

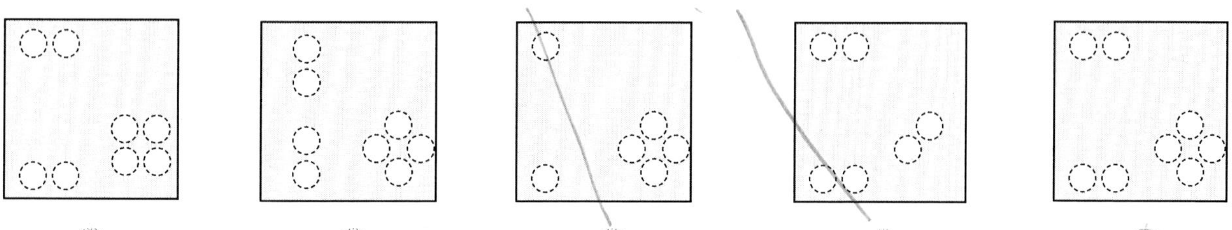

A B C D E

Directions: What answer choice should you put in the place of the question mark so that both sides of the equal sign total the same amount?

17/20

1

34 = 2 x ?

(A) 17 (B) 32 (C) 16 (D) 18 (E) 27

2

4 x 9 = 59 - ?

18 x 2 = 36

59 - 36 = 23

(A) 46 (B) 13 (C) 33 (D) 36 (E) 23

3

12 + 9 = 7 x ?

(A) 21 (B) 3 (C) 14 (D) 13 (E) 4

4

12 X ? = 60

12 x 5 = 150

(A) 72 (B) 6 (C) 54 (D) 5 (E) 48

5

3 + ? = ◆

2 + ◆ = 5

(A) 5 (B) 0 (C) 10 (D) 3 (E) 1

6

$63 \div 9 = \boxed{?} \div 10$

(A) 72 (B) 63 (C) 70 (D) 6 (E) 7

7

$\boxed{?} \div 5 = 4 \times 5$

(A) 95 (B) 5 (C) 4 (D) 100 (E) 20

8

$12 \times 4 = 12 + \boxed{?}$

(A) 26 (B) 36 (C) 16 (D) 48 (E) 4

9

$1 + \boxed{?} = \blacklozenge$

$6 - \blacklozenge = 3$

(A) 1 (B) 3 (C) 6 (D) 4 (E) 2

10

$6 \times 11 = 19 + \boxed{?}$

(A) 19 (B) 47 (C) 37 (D) 57 (E) 66

11

$12 \times 2 = \boxed{?} \div 3$

(A) 14 (B) 8 (C) 72 (D) 48 (E) 24

12

$14 \times 3 = \boxed{?} \times 6$

(A) 9 (B) 17 (C) 36 (D) 7 (E) 42

13

$3 + \boxed{?} = ◆$

$2 + ◆ = 10$

(A) 11 (B) 2 (C) 8 (D) 15 (E) 5

14

$2 \times \boxed{?} = ◆$

$2 + ◆ = 18$

(A) 14 (B) 16 (C) 10 (D) 9 (E) 8

15

$\boxed{?} + 13 = 2 \times ◆$

$2 = ◆ - 10$

(A) 12 (B) 11 (C) 24 (D) 13 (E) 14

16

[?] + 6 = 28 ÷ ◆

2 = ◆ - 2

(A) 2 (B) 3 (C) 7 (D) 1 (E) 4

17

[?] - 10 = ◆ x 5

● = ◆ ÷ 2

● = 3

(A) 3 (B) 50 (C) 40 (D) 30 (E) 6

18

[?] - 10 = ◆ x 4

● = ◆ x 2

● = 8

(A) 40 (B) 36 (C) 16 (D) 8 (E) 26

19

[?] = ◆ + 8

10 = ◆ - ●

● = 2

(A) 12 (B) 20 (C) 10 (D) 30 (E) 8

20

[?] = ◆ + 7

7 = ◆ + ●

● = 3

(A) 5 (B) 11 (C) 2 (D) 3 (E) 4

Directions: Look at the first two sets of numbers. Come up with a rule that both sets follow. Take this rule to figure out which answer choice goes in the place of the question mark.

1 [40 → 16] [52 → 28] [61 → ?]

(A) 28 (B) 16 (C) 27 (D) 37 (E) 85

2 [33 → 72] [41 → 80] [25 → ?]

(A) 64 (B) 93 (C) 88 (D) 54 (E) 74

3 [27 → 53] [17 → 43] [46 → ?]

(A) 20 (B) 64 (C) 33 (D) 72 (E) 62

4 [11 → 99] [10 → 90] [12 → ?]

(A) 3 (B) 109 (C) 21 (D) 89 (E) 108

5 [34 → 17] [54 → 27] [40 → ?]

(A) 37 (B) 80 (C) 20 (D) 2 (E) 22

6 [4 → 16] [6 → 36] [7 → ?]

(A) 9 (B) 49 (C) 46 (D) 28 (E) 14

7 [1 1/2 → 2] [1 1/4 → 1 3/4] [0 → ?]

(A) 1/4 (B) 3/4 (C) 1/2 (D) 1/3 (E) 2/7

8 [0.45 → 4.5] [0.06 → 0.6] [10 → ?]

(A) 100 (B) 1 (C) 10.1 (D) 10.101 (E) 1.01

9 [1/4 → 2/8] [1/2 → 5/10] [1/3 → ?]

(A) 1/6 (B) 4/12 (C) 6/12 (D) 6/10 (E) 2/5

10 [10 → 1] [100 → 10] [0.9 → ?]

(A) 90.9 (B) 0.909 (C) 90.1 (D) 0.09 (E) 90

11 [2 → 3] [4 → 7] [5 → ?]

(A) 6 (B) 8 (C) 11 (D) 10 (E) 9

12 [3 → 8] [6 → 17] [5 → ?]

(A) 2 (B) 8 (C) 14 (D) 10 (E) 16

13 [12 → 25] [15 → 31] [17 → ?]

(A) 20 (B) 35 (C) 33 (D) 37 (E) 23

14 [8 → 41] [10 → 51] [7 → ?]

(A) 71 (B) 13 (C) 48 (D) 61 (E) 36

15 [12 → 38] [9 → 29] [10 → ?]

(A) 42 (B) 18 (C) 28 (D) 32 (E) 30

16 [10 → 41] [8 → 33] [9 → ?]

(A) 22 (B) 14 (C) 37 (D) 30 (E) 25

17 [15 → 32] [20 → 42] [9 → ?]

(A) 52 (B) 13 (C) 20 (D) 16 (E) 18

18 [10 → 4] [4 → 1] [12 → ?]

(A) 3 (B) 5 (C) 6 (D) 9 (E) 10

19 [6 → 2] [14 → 6] [30 → ?]

(A) 22 (B) 51 (C) 16 (D) 8 (E) 14

20 [38 → 20] [12 → 7] [28 → ?]

(A) 81 (B) 41 (C) 17 (D) 15 (E) 29

21 [30 → 9] [45 → 14] [27 → ?]

(A) 8 (B) 6 (C) 10 (D) 19 (E) 20

22 [34 → 18] [28 → 15] [50 → ?]

(A) 12 (B) 15 (C) 26 (D) 76 (E) 24

23 [12 → 5] [27 → 10] [36 → ?]

(A) 19 (B) 13 (C) 15 (D) 10 (E) 11

24 [8 → 3] [18 → 8] [20 → ?]

(A) 0 (B) 9 (C) 2 (D) 11 (E) 10

Directions: Which answer choice would complete the pattern?

1 59 2 70 2 81 2 ?

(A) 22 (B) 12 (C) 71 (D) 2 (E) 92

2 30 32 34 33 35 37 36 38 40 ?

(A) 39 (B) 40 (C) 43 (D) 37 (E) 30

3 70.01 70.10 70.19 70.28 70.37 70.46 ?

(A) 70.55 (B) 70.64 (C) 75.05 (D) 70.09 (E) 71.36

4 12 15 21 28 31 37 44 47 53 ?

(A) 56 (B) 46 (C) 60 (D) 50 (E) 70

5 80 160 40 80 20 40 10 20 5 ?

(A) 1 (B) 24 (C) 7 (D) 25 (E) 10

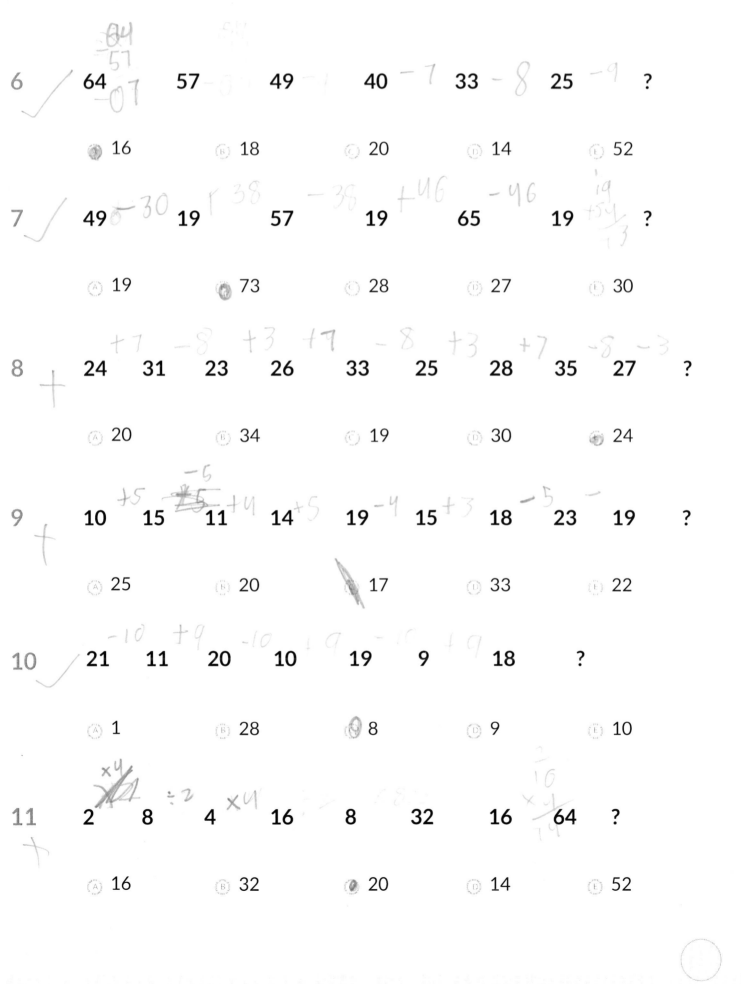

6 **64 57 49 40 33 25 ?**

(A) 16 (B) 18 (C) 20 (D) 14 (E) 52

7 **49 19 57 19 65 19 ?**

(A) 19 (B) 73 (C) 28 (D) 27 (E) 30

8 **24 31 23 26 33 25 28 35 27 ?**

(A) 20 (B) 34 (C) 19 (D) 30 (E) 24

9 **10 15 11 14 19 15 18 23 19 ?**

(A) 25 (B) 20 (C) 17 (D) 33 (E) 22

10 **21 11 20 10 19 9 18 ?**

(A) 1 (B) 28 (C) 8 (D) 9 (E) 10

11 **2 8 4 16 8 32 16 64 ?**

(A) 16 (B) 32 (C) 20 (D) 14 (E) 52

12 4 8 16 8 16 32 16 32 64 ?

(A) 32 (B) 4 (C) 16 (D) 8 (E) 12

13 3 6 12 11 22 44 43 ?

(A) 20 (B) 40 (C) 42 (D) 86 (E) 45

14 0.06 0.11 0.09 0.14 0.12 0.17 0.15 ?

(A) 0.051 (B) 0.13 (C) 2.02 (D) 0.20 (E) 0.02

15 2 3 5 8 11 15 20 25 31 ?

(A) 41 (B) 38 (C) 15 (D) 24 (E) 39

16 20 10 5 40 20 10 80 40 ?

(A) 2 (B) 4 (C) 10 (D) 80 (E) 20

17 50 49 47 44 41 37 32 27 21 ?

(A) 14 (B) 25 (C) 28 (D) 35 (E) 10

- Cut out pages 91-94 (the Answer Key pages).
- Write your child's answer in the blank space (_____).
- At the end of each group of questions, total the number of questions answered correctly. This will provide a general overview of strengths/weaknesses according to COGAT® question type.

Verbal Analogies, p. 10, Practice Test 1 (Workbook Format) Questions Answered Correctly: ______ out of 22

_____ 1. E.
_____ 2. B. 2D shape > 3D version of this shape
_____ 3. B. Job > the final product of what someone who has the job designs (drawings is not correct because it is not a final product; buildings is a final product)
_____ 4. D. Planet > distance from the sun
_____ 5. E. Towering means ***very*** tall. Terrifying means ***very*** scary. (Spooky is not correct - it does not mean ***very*** scary.)
_____ 6. E. Temperature is measured by a thermometer. Distance is measured by an odometer.
_____ 7. B. There are 3 performers in a trio. There are 3 wheels on a tricycle.
_____ 8. C. Paper is made from trees. Flour is made from grains.
_____ 9. D. Glass feels smooth. Pavement feels rough.
_____ 10. C. People go to a casino to gamble. People go to a restaurant to dine.
_____ 11. C. These are homophones. (Words that sound the same but have different spellings/meanings.)
_____ 12. A. Synonyms
_____ 13. E. Opposites
_____ 14. D. A goose's form of movement is a waddle. A snake's is a slither.
_____ 15. C. Profession > A material this profession works with and the main material used to make things
_____ 16. B. Ferocious means very fierce. Ancient means very old.
_____ 17. A. A helmet's purpose is to protect. A vehicle's purpose is to transport (things/people).
_____ 18. E. Present tense > past tense.
_____ 19. B. A debate is moderated by a neutral moderator. A game is monitored by a neutral referee.
_____ 20. D. To put things in numerical order, numbers are used. For chronological order, times (or, dates) are used.
_____ 21. E. A teacher is a type of occupation. A ferry is a type of vessel.
_____ 22. C. A novel is a long story. A marathon is a long run.

Verbal Classification, p. 13, Practice Test 1 (Workbook Format) Questions Answered Correctly: ______ out of 22

_____ 1. D. bodies of water
_____ 2. C. buildings -or- large rooms in buildings for events
_____ 3. D. measurement units
_____ 4. B. adjectives that can describe something being done quickly
_____ 5. A. planets
_____ 6. D. having to do w/ money
_____ 7. D. used for storage
_____ 8. E. having to do with the middle of something
_____ 9. B. having to do with above average intelligence
_____ 10. A. amounts of time
_____ 11. B. appliances used to heat things
_____ 12. C. countries
_____ 13. E. food growing above ground
_____ 14. B. used to keep something safe
_____ 15. D. health-related professions
_____ 16. C. landforms
_____ 17. B. government officials who are elected (or, selected)
_____ 18. D. used to describe not having enough
_____ 19. E. having to do with things that are the same in some way
_____ 20. C. having to do with frequency
_____ 21. D. having to do with getting smaller
_____ 22. A. having to do with no longer being together

Sentence Completion, p. 16, Practice Test 1 (Workbook Format) Questions Answered Correctly: ______ out of 22

_____ 1. D. advise = to give advice about
_____ 2. D. abrupt = sudden (and not expected)
_____ 3. B. transfer = move from one place to another
_____ 4. A. origin = place/point where something started / where it was from
_____ 5. C. genuine = a thing that's what it's said to be/real
_____ 6. A. adequate = enough of something
_____ 7. B. assemble = to put together parts
_____ 8. C. compilation = something that's put together by bringing together separate/different things
_____ 9. B. contribution = a payment or a gift / donation
_____ 10. D. status = something's ranking/standing
_____ 11. B. subtle = not obvious or easy to see
_____ 12. E. capture = to take into your control; notorious = famous for something bad
_____ 13. E. impact = effect; ability = having the means to do something/to be able to do something
_____ 14. C. result in = cause to happen; alternative = something that's possible as another choice
_____ 15. E. concur = agree
_____ 16. B. potential = to have or show the ability to make something in the future; generate = produce
_____ 17. D. phase = a part/period of an event with different parts; consists of = made up of
_____ 18. A. capacity = the most something can hold
_____ 19. E. detect = to sense/discover; virtually = almost
_____ 20. C. equate = to think of something as the same as something else.
_____ 21. E. adversary = opponent; tactic = an action or method used to achieve something
_____ 22. B. tradition = a long-held custom or belief; obscure = not known

Figure Classification, p. 21, Practice Test 1 (Workbook Format) Questions Answered Correctly: ______ out of 18

_____ 1. E.
_____ 2. A. arrows pointing right
_____ 3. D. design alternates solid & curvy lines
_____ 4. E. inside the larger circle, a smaller circle & a diamond are opposite each other
_____ 5. C. 3 shapes, and 1 of them is a circle OR there is only 1 gray circle
_____ 6. B. each group of 3 shapes has a shape filled with either dashed lines, curvy lines, or gray
_____ 7. A. in group of 2 same shapes, bottom shape rotates 90° counter-clockwise
_____ 8. C. 3 shapes
_____ 9. D. combos of heart-square-hexagon
_____ 10. B. small circle is in the shape's corner
_____ 11. D. shapes divided in 2 parts: 1/4 & 3/4 (or 3/4 &1/4)
_____ 12. A. half of shape is shaded (with dots)

_____ 13. C. the inside designs of the arrow (darker gray-lighter gray-gray dots) remain in the same order as the arrow rotates and the arrow shape is the same size
_____ 14. B. shapes with rounded corners
_____ 15. D. Inside square are 3 shapes: octagon that's next to parallelogram and a star that is not
_____ 16. E. groups of lines with one curved line _____ 17. A. 6-sided shape with a square in the middle
_____ 18. A. tic-tac-toe with hexagons (3 in a row) -OR- hexagon in the middle of shape group
_____ 19. B. order of shapes: pentagon (5 sided shape) - parallelogram - oval

Figure Analogies, p. 28, Practice Test 1 (Workbook Format) Questions Answered Correctly: _____ out of 19
_____ 1. B.
_____ 2. D. second box has the right shape of the 2 shapes in the first box - this shape changes to gray
_____ 3. E. group of ovals flips & 1 oval is added
_____ 4. B. top shape goes inside bottom shape & gets bigger; middle shape goes inside & rotates 90° clockwise.
_____ 5. C. in top set, circle design switches from solid gray to dashed lines; the lower left "pac-man" shape changes to the curved figure - it is in the upper right and the design inside has changed from dashed lines to solid gray; in the bottom, the reverse occurs; the circle changes from dashed lines to solid gray, the gray "pac-man" changes to the curved figure, and changes its position & design (solid gray to dashed lines); no change w/ trapezoid.
_____ 6. D. from left to right, larger shape will have 2 less sides, smaller shape will have +1 side; colors of large & small shapes reverse
_____ 7. A. white shape increases & gray shape decreases with smaller version on top of larger version
_____ 8. B. small white shape inside large gray shape turns gray & rotates 90° clockwise
_____ 9. C. top half of shape group in the second box
_____ 10. E. these switch: upper left, bottom right; Upper right, bottom left
_____ 11. D. upper left figure rotates 180° to face down; Upper right & lower right shapes switch and the new upper right becomes dotted
_____ 12. A. the shorter bar with horizontal stripes becomes solid gray; middle white bar remains white; the longer bar with curved lines remains with curved lines; then, the group of 3 bars rotates 180°; in the answer, horizontal stripes become solid gray, curved lines remain curved lines, white remains white, then the group of 3 bars rotates 180°
_____ 13. B. 2 horizontal lines are added inside the shape and the vertical bar extends outside the shape
_____ 14. A. larger shape from first box gets smaller, becomes darker gray & moves where the 3 lines meet
_____ 15. B. shapes (diamond & pentagon) are divided into 4 equal parts; in the first box, 1/4 of the shape is positioned inside the shape; the small inside shape moves to fill the missing 1/4 of the larger shape and turns gray
_____ 16. E. the outside shape becomes the inside shape, gets smaller, and switches color; the inside shape becomes the outside shape, gets bigger, and switches color; the middle shape remains the middle shape, gets smaller, and switches color
_____ 17. C. left shape goes inside middle shape, then moves to right side of the line; the right shape moves to left side of the line
_____ 18. B. left side shows half of a shape with a star in the lower left corner; right side shows the other half of the shape, the star moves to the upper right corner, a triangle is added in the middle, and a line is added across the middle of the shape half
_____ 19. D. shapes are divided into 4 equal parts; there's a group of 4 shapes on the left and another group of 4 on the right; the sections that are filled in with dark gray change from the left group of 4 shapes to the right group of 4 shapes, like this: lower left > lower right; upper left > upper right; lower right> lower left; upper right > upper left

Paper Folding, p. 35, Practice Test 1 (Workbook Format Questions Answered Correctly: _____ out of 17
_____ 1. D _____ 2. E _____ 3. D _____ 4. C _____ 5. C _____ 6. B _____ 7. C _____ 8. A _____ 9. C
_____ 10. B _____ 11. D _____ 12. D _____ 13. E _____ 14. A _____ 15. B _____ 16. D _____ 17. C

Number Puzzles, p. 41, Practice Test 1 (Workbook Format) Questions Answered Correctly: _____ out of 17
_____ 1. C _____ 2. E _____ 3. D _____ 4. B _____ 5. A _____ 6. B _____ 7. B _____ 8. D _____ 9. A _____ 10. E
_____ 11. B _____ 12. D _____ 13. C _____ 14. D _____ 15. A _____ 16. B _____ 17. E

Number Analogies, p. 45, Practice Test 1 (Workbook Format) Questions Answered Correctly: _____ out of 23
_____ 1. D. -8 _____ 2. A. +9 _____ 3. C. ÷ 7 _____ 4. E. x8 _____ 5. C. half _____ 6. B. squared
_____ 7. C. +1/4 _____ 8. A. ÷ 10 _____ 9. B. same _____ 10. D. ÷ 10 _____ 11. E. -13 _____ 12. C.+32
_____ 13. B. x2 then +1 _____ 14. E. x5 then +1 _____ 15. D. x3 then +2 _____ 16. C. x4 then +1
_____ 17. C. x2 then +2 _____ 18. B. x5 then +1 _____ 19. E. x4 then +1 _____ 20. D. ÷2 then +1
_____ 21. A. ÷3 then +1 _____ 22. C. ÷2 then +1 _____ 23. B. ÷3 then +1

Number Series, p. 50, Practice Test 1 (Workbook Format) Questions Answered Correctly: _____ out of 23
_____ 1.D. -8 _____ 2. E. x2 previous number
_____ 3. D. +16 _____ 4. B. +1, +7, +1, +7, continues _____ 5. A. +2,+3,+4,+5,+6,+7,+8 _____ 6. C. -2,-3,-2,-3,etc.
_____ 7. A. begins w/5, every other number is 5; then, starting with 11, every other number is +1
_____ 8. B. -8,-7,-6,-5,-4,-3,-2 _____ 9. A. +2,-3,+2,-3,+2,-3, etc. OR #s in spots 1,3,5,7 & 2,4,6,8 decrease by 1 each time
_____ 10. B. +3, +6, +7, etc. _____ 11. D. div by 2 _____ 12. E. x4, div 2, x4, div 2, etc. _____ 13. C. +2,+2,-1, etc.
_____ 14. A. +0.05 _____ 15. E. -5,-6,-7, etc.
_____ 16. D. begins w/7, every other number is 7; then, starting with 18, every other number is +4
_____ 17. E. +5,-8,+2, etc. _____ 18. B. +6,-9,+4, etc _____ 19. C. -10,+8.-2, etc _____ 20. E. -7,+9,-4, etc
_____ 21. A. every other number is 39; with 64 every other number +8
_____ 22. D. +1, +1, -1, +3, +3, -3, +4, +4, -4 _____ 23. A. x2, x2, div by 2, x2, x2, div by 2

Verbal Analogies, p. 55, Practice Test 2 Questions Answered Correctly: _____ out of 20

_____ 1. D. Cells make up a body. Words make up a book. _____ 2. C. The first thing flows inside the second.
_____ 3. E. The second word is a "type" of the first word. (A cello is a type of instrument. A koala is a type of species.)
_____ 4. A. Something people use today for a purpose > something people used in the past for that same purpose
_____ 5. C. Word > word spelled backwards _____ 6. C. Opposites
_____ 7. B. Blocks joined together form a wall. Thread joined together make cloth.
_____ 8. A. Homophones (words that sound the same but have different spellings/meanings).
_____ 9. D. Inches put together make up a foot. Decades put together make up a century.
_____ 10. A. It is a translator's job to take information & produce a translation. A judge's job is to take information to produce a ruling.
_____ 11. E. Synonyms _____ 12. B. A safe is used to store valuables. A silo is used to store grain.
_____ 13. E. A face is protected by a mask. Candy is protected by a wrapper.
_____ 14. B. The top of the mountain is the summit. The top of the wave is the crest.
_____ 15. C. Opposites _____ 16. B. Excess heat causes a burn. Excess rain causes a flood.
_____ 17. E. When something decreases in size, it shrinks. When something has a decreased amount of light, it dims.
_____ 18. D. Opposites _____ 19. A. Something dry lacks moisture. Something that's borderless lacks a boundary.
_____ 20. B. Biology is a branch of science. Geometry is a branch of mathematics.

Verbal Classification, p. 57, Practice Test 2 Questions Answered Correctly: _____ out of 20

_____ 1. D. adjectives of the world's continents _____ 2. E. body organs _____ 3. A. time measurements
_____ 4. C. primates _____ 5. E. shades of red _____ 6. B. verbs associated with teaching
_____ 7. C. non-fiction book types _____ 8. E. used to travel from one place to another
_____ 9. D. verbs associated with going up _____ 10. C. adjectives associated with being very surprised
_____ 11. A. adjectives associated with not having enough water/moisture
_____ 12. C. words associated with being completely different than something else
_____ 13. D. workers trained to respond in emergency situations
_____ 14. B. the lower part of a building/land mass
_____ 15. A. verbs involved with guessing what will happen in the future _____ 16. E. feelings associated with sleepiness
_____ 17. C. people who are often on the same side _____ 18. C. rivers
_____ 19. A. enclosed areas used for storage _____ 20. D. ways to classify things

Sentence Completion, p. 59, Practice Test 2 Questions Answered Correctly: _____ out of 20

_____ 1. B. valid = acceptable under the law or acceptable because of certain rules
_____ 2. D. credible = something that's able to be believed
_____ 3. E. decrease = to go down _____ 4. A. to make something known (that before was not known)
_____ 5. C. meticulous = being very precise/careful
_____ 6. A. alleges = to claim that someone has done something wrong (usually without enough proof)
_____ 7. B. conditional = something that will happen only if something else happens
_____ 8. D. factor = something that leads to (or, influences) a result
_____ 9. E. criteria = something used to make a decision or to judge something
_____ 10. A. correlate = to have a close connection with something else
_____ 11. E. isolate = to keep something in a place that's separated from everything else
_____ 12. B. convert = to change something into something else so that it can be used in a different way
_____ 13. C. distinct = different from everything else (that is in some way similar to it)
_____ 14. D. method = a procedure for doing something; modified = made partial changes to something
_____ 15. B. implied = said/communicated something in an indirect way; exaggerated = said something is bigger/better than it really is
_____ 16. D. aspect = a part of something; emphasize = to give extra attention to something
_____ 17. B. structure = something that has been built; secure = safe, protected
_____ 18. E. precise = exact; approximate = close to what it should be, but not exact
_____ 19. C. transmitted = passed on / sent ; susceptible = more easily affected by something
_____ 20. A. approached = got closer to a place; exhibit = to show

Figure Analogies, p. 63, Practice Test 2 Questions Answered Correctly: _____ out of 18

_____ 1. A. # of arrow points > # of shape sides
_____ 2. D. # of lines with circles on the end increases by 1 & the group rotates 90° clockwise
_____ 3. E. 1/4 of diamond shape (which is a triangle) is removed
_____ 4. B. the gray of the inner shape & the curvy lines of the outer shape switch to outer shape & inner shape, respectively; outer shape adds +1 side
_____ 5. C. 2 shapes come together & the inner designs switch (dotted lines & dark gray); bottom shape flips vertically
_____ 6. B. small shapes placed in each corner of large shape & these shapes have +1 more side than the larger shape
_____ 7. E. shapes divided in half & the middle shape flips upside down in 2nd box
_____ 8. E. lighter shape 'flips' down, darker shape added on top that's facing the original position of the first shape
_____ 9. C. in the 1st box, note the location of the thin darker gray section; in 2nd box, the base of lighter "V" shape is where the middle of this thin darker gray section was in the 1st box; also, in the 2nd box, the larger shape becomes darker
_____ 10. A. square & arrow figure rotates 180° & 3 stars switch colors
_____ 11. D. light gray sections become dark gray & vice versa

continued

_____ 12. D. on top, white rectangle with 1/4 filled w/ darker gray becomes light gray circle with same amount (1/4) filled; on the bottom, lighter gray rectangle with 1/2 filled w/ darker gray becomes white circle w/ same amount (1/2) filled; note that the design & quantity of the inside lines must be the same also
_____ 13. B. lighter gray becomes solid lines (choice B is only choice with this); in top set darker gray became dotted lines & this reverses in bottom set - dotted lines become darker gray
_____ 14. B. top shape goes inside bottom shape & gets bigger; middle shape goes inside & rotates 90° clockwise
_____ 15. E. in 2nd box, half of middle shape is covered; the lighter gray section comes to the front while the white and darker gray "quarters" switch positions with the lighter gray section; the covered middle shape switches from white to gray on top & from gray to white on bottom
_____ 16. C. middle shape gets bigger & top shape goes inside; bottom shape rotates 90° counterclockwise & goes inside and turns gray
_____ 17. D. color of large square changes from dark gray to white; top shape (pentagon in top set, "L" shape in bottom set) rotates 180°; lower shapes (circle, octagon in top set; diamond, arrow in bottom set) switch sides -and- the bottom right shape (octagon in top set, arrow in bottom set) changes from filled with dotted lines to dark gray
____ 18. B. group of figures shows 3 "half" shapes; from left to right, largest half has 5 sides, then 3 sides; middle half points down, then up; smallest half has rounded corners, then a version of this same half, but with straight corners

<u>Figure Classification, p. 69, Practice Test 2</u> Questions Answered Correctly: _____ out of 18

_____ 1. E. dotted lines inside
_____ 2. A. straight/angled corners (not rounded)
_____ 3. C. in group of 2 shapes, right shape has 1 more side than the left shape
_____ 4. A. 3 down/1 up triangle
_____ 5. B. circles divided into equal parts
_____ 6. B. inside larger shape are 2 small, vertically-aligned diamonds with same color
_____ 7. D. star and trapezoid are beside each other inside oval
_____ 8. E. shapes are wider than they are tall
_____ 9. E. group has 1 up arrow, 1 "U"- shaped crescent, 1 tri-arrow pointing up; 1 shape is darker gray, 1 filled w/ lines, 1 lighter gray
_____ 10. A. as shape group rotates, the smaller shapes stay in same position within the shape group
_____ 11. A. shape filled with lines has 1 more side than white shape
_____ 12. D. group has 1 octagon, 1 heart, 1 hexagon; 1 dark gray, 1 filled with small dotted lines, 1 white
_____ 13. C. triangle and circle are same color with a different colored square in middle
_____ 14. A. shapes divided in half, positioned with lines going upper right to lower left
_____ 15. C. symmetrical shapes
_____ 16. B. on the left and right side of larger shape are smaller halves of the same shape
_____ 17. E. 1 heart & tic-tac-toe with stars
_____ 18. E. 1 darker gray & 1 lighter gray opposite each other; 4 sections of circle have different designs

<u>Paper Folding, p. 75, Practice Test 2</u> Questions Answered Correctly: _____ out of 15

_____ 1. E _____ 2. A _____ 3. C _____ 4. E _____ 5. A _____ 6. D _____ 7. C _____ 8. B _____ 9. D
_____ 10. A _____ 11. E _____ 12. B _____ 13. C _____ 14. C _____ 15. E

<u>Number Puzzles, p. 80, Practice Test 2</u> Questions Answered Correctly: _____ out of 20

_____ 1. A _____ 2. E _____ 3. B _____ 4. D _____ 5. B _____ 6. C _____ 7. D _____ 8. B _____ 9. E
_____ 10. B _____ 11. C _____ 12. D _____ 13. E _____ 14. E _____ 15. B _____ 16. D _____ 17. C _____ 18. E
_____ 19. B _____ 20. B

<u>Number Analogies, p. 84, Practice Test 2</u> Questions Answered Correctly: _____ out of 24

_____ 1. D. -24 _____ 2. A. +39 _____ 3. D. +26 _____ 4. E. x9 _____ 5. C. half
_____ 6. B. squared _____ 7. C. +1/2 _____ 8. A. x 10 _____ 9. B. same _____ 10. D. ÷ 10
_____ 11. E. x2 then -1 _____ 12. C. x3 then -1 _____ 13. B. x2 then +1 _____ 14. E. x5 then +1
_____ 15. D. x3 then +2 _____ 16. C. x4 then +1 _____ 17. C. x2 then +2 _____ 18. B. ÷2 then -1
_____ 19. E. ÷2 then -1 _____ 20. D. ÷2 then +1 _____ 21. A. ÷3 then -1 _____ 22. C. ÷2 then +1
_____ 23. B. ÷3 then +1 _____ 24. B. ÷2 then -1

<u>Number Series, p. 88, Practice Test 2</u> Questions Answered Correctly: _____ out of 17

_____ 1. E. alternates +11 & the number 2 _____ 2. A. +2,+2,-1; +2,+2,-1 (repeats) _____ 3. A. +0.09
_____ 4. C. +3,+6,+7 (repeats) _____ 5. E. x2, div by 4 (repeats) _____ 6. A. -7,-8,-9 (repeats)
_____ 7. B. alternates +8 & the number 19 _____ 8. D. +7,-8,+3 (repeats) _____ 9. E. +5,-4,+3 (repeats)
_____ 10. C. -10, +9 _____ 11. B. x4, div by 2 (repeats) OR every other number is multiplied by 2
_____ 12. A. x2,x2, div by 2 _____ 13. D. x2,x2,-1 (repeats)
_____ 14. D. +0.05, -0.02 (repeats) _____ 15. B +1,+2,+3; +3,+4,+5; +5,+6,+7
_____ 16. E. div by 2, div by 2, x8 (repeats) _____ 17. A. -1,-2,-3; -3,-4,-5; -5,-6,-7

PRACTICE TEST 2 NOTES

- Our suggestion: have your student complete Practice Test 2 on his/her own (do not tell whether the answers are correct or not until the test is completed).
- The time limit for each of the 9 question sections (Verbal Analogies, Verbal Classification, etc.) is approximately 10 minutes each.

Our suggestion: do a group of 3 question sections per day.

- Day 1, Verbal: 10 minutes each for Verbal Analogies, Verbal Classification, Sentence Completion = 30 minutes total
- Day 2, Non-Verbal: 10 minutes each for Figure Analogies, Figure Classification, Paper Folding = 30 minutes total
- Day 3, Quantitative: 10 minutes each for Number Analogies, Number Puzzles, Number Series = 30 minutes total
- After your student is finished, on your own (without your child), go through the answer key by question type to see which answers were correct/incorrect.

Verbal Analogies, p.55

1	A	B	C	D	E
2	A	B	C	D	E
3	A	B	C	D	E
4	A	B	C	D	E
5	A	B	C	D	E
6	A	B	C	D	E
7	A	B	C	D	E
8	A	B	C	D	E
9	A	B	C	D	E
10	A	B	C	D	E
11	A	B	C	D	E
12	A	B	C	D	E
13	A	B	C	D	E
14	A	B	C	D	E
15	A	B	C	D	E
16	A	B	C	D	E
17	A	B	C	D	E
18	A	B	C	D	E
19	A	B	C	D	E
20	A	B	C	D	E

Verbal Classification, p.57

1	A	B	C	D	E
2	A	B	C	D	E
3	A	B	C	D	E
4	A	B	C	D	E
5	A	B	C	D	E
6	A	B	C	D	E
7	A	B	C	D	E
8	A	B	C	D	E
9	A	B	C	D	E
10	A	B	C	D	E
11	A	B	C	D	E
12	A	B	C	D	E
13	A	B	C	D	E
14	A	B	C	D	E
15	A	B	C	D	E
16	A	B	C	D	E
17	A	B	C	D	E
18	A	B	C	D	E
19	A	B	C	D	E
20	A	B	C	D	E

Sentence Completion, p.59

1	A	B	C	D	E
2	A	B	C	D	E
3	A	B	C	D	E
4	A	B	C	D	E
5	A	B	C	D	E
6	A	B	C	D	E
7	A	B	C	D	E
8	A	B	C	D	E
9	A	B	C	D	E
10	A	B	C	D	E
11	A	B	C	D	E
12	A	B	C	D	E
13	A	B	C	D	E
14	A	B	C	D	E
15	A	B	C	D	E
16	A	B	C	D	E
17	A	B	C	D	E
18	A	B	C	D	E
19	A	B	C	D	E
20	A	B	C	D	E

Figure Analogies, p.63

1	A	B	C	D	E
2	A	B	C	D	E
3	A	B	C	D	E
4	A	B	C	D	E
5	A	B	C	D	E
6	A	B	C	D	E
7	A	B	C	D	E
8	A	B	C	D	E
9	A	B	C	D	E
10	A	B	C	D	E
11	A	B	C	D	E
12	A	B	C	D	E
13	A	B	C	D	E
14	A	B	C	D	E
15	A	B	C	D	E
16	A	B	C	D	E
17	A	B	C	D	E
18	A	B	C	D	E

#	Figure Classification, p.69	Paper Folding, p.75	Number Puzzles, p.80	Number Analogies, p.84	Number Series, p.88
1	A B C D E	A B C D E	A B C D E	A B C D E	A B C D E
2	A B C D E	A B C D E	A B C D E	A B C D E	A B C D E
3	A B C D E	A B C D E	A B C D E	A B C D E	A B C D E
4	A B C D E	A B C D E	A B C D E	A B C D E	A B C D E
5	A B C D E	A B C D E	A B C D E	A B C D E	A B C D E
6	A B C D E	A B C D E	A B C D E	A B C D E	A B C D E
7	A B C D E	A B C D E	A B C D E	A B C D E	A B C D E
8	A B C D E	A B C D E	A B C D E	A B C D E	A B C D E
9	A B C D E	A B C D E	A B C D E	A B C D E	A B C D E
10	A B C D E	A B C D E	A B C D E	A B C D E	A B C D E
11	A B C D E	A B C D E	A B C D E	A B C D E	A B C D E
12	A B C D E	A B C D E	A B C D E	A B C D E	A B C D E
13	A B C D E	A B C D E	A B C D E	A B C D E	A B C D E
14	A B C D E	A B C D E	A B C D E	A B C D E	A B C D E
15	A B C D E	A B C D E	A B C D E	A B C D E	A B C D E
16	A B C D E		A B C D E	A B C D E	A B C D E
17	A B C D E		A B C D E	A B C D E	A B C D E
18	A B C D E		A B C D E	A B C D E	
19			A B C D E	A B C D E	
20			A B C D E	A B C D E	
21				A B C D E	
22				A B C D E	
23				A B C D E	
24				A B C D E	

9 781733 113236